SMALL BUSINESS SURVIVAL 101

SMALL BUSINESS
SURVIVAL
101

*Principles for Fail
Proofing Your Business*

TOM PEASE

NEW YORK

SMALL BUSINESS SURVIVAL 101
Principles for Fail Proofing Your Business

ISBN 978-1-61448-790-6 paperback
ISBN 978-1-61448-791-3 eBook
Library of Congress Control Number: 2013944422

Morgan James Publishing
The Entrepreneurial Publisher
5 Penn Plaza, 23rd Floor,
New York City, New York 10001
(212) 655-5470 office • (516) 908-4496 fax
www.MorganJamesPublishing.com

Cover Design by:
Chris Treccani
www.3dogdesign.net

Interior Design by:
Bonnie Bushman
bonnie@caboodlegraphics.com

In an effort to support local communities, raise awareness and funds, Morgan James Publishing donates a percentage of all book sales for the life of each book to Habitat for Humanity Peninsula and Greater Williamsburg.

Get involved today, visit
www.MorganJamesBuilds.com.

Habitat
for Humanity®
Peninsula and
Greater Williamsburg
Building Partner

CONTENTS

Acknowledgements

I dedicate this to my employees who live this life with me as well as those I employed. You have comprised the majority of my life and helped create something to be proud of. I love my mission as the keeper of it all.

I thank God for the business ability and the wisdom to do the right things. He has bailed me many times. Thanks to my wife Cindy for enduring the unique ups and downs of a business owner's life. Your stabilizing influence has helped keep crises from getting overwhelming.

Thanks to Bridget DiCello for her suggestions on this book. Thanks to Ed Horrell for inspiring me to write my first book and now there is another. To James Overstreet, Executive Editor of *The Daily News,* my thanks for my business column which improved my writing.

I thank my beloved children, Parker and Lacey, who worked for their Dad and lived to tell about it. Thanks to Parker for eight years of revenue production and support of his father. Lacey has since started her own company.

Thanks to: Dad Tom, 89, living legend with Bronze Star and two Purple Hearts, parachuting skill learned with the 101ˢᵗ Airborne and member of the Greatest Generation, who bequeathed mental toughness, morale rightness, model fatherhood, and businessman's blood. Brother Mike, for his enthusiastic encouragement for my writing projects. My loyal dog Moe, for his lessons and summations. My deceased mother Jo, who lived as an unattainable example. The fine managers of my company, especially VP Cindy McLarty, Director of Service Theo Harris, and Director of Sales Stuart Blessing. Special mention to Paul Ginn my former VP. All of you know what it is really about.

Preface

I have owned an office equipment dealership in Memphis for 32 years and counting. I have faced extinction, embezzlement, malfeasance, several recessions, poor cash flow, employee sicknesses, personal discouragement, partnership problems, unrelenting competition, a few lawsuits, but no mutinies, and a decline in my industry. Even so, I have had an answer for it all and earned a good living in the process. I hope to give you the benefit of this experience, especially how to stay in business and deal with trouble.

Why do some companies stay in business and others don't? The Small Business Administration says 46% of small businesses fail within four years and 69% within seven. What is going wrong in these scandalous figures which evidence so much wasted time, jobs, and capital? The answers are in *Small Business Survival 101*. You can avoid being a statistic by deploying Small Business Survival 101 principles. The need for better formation is great. Applying SBA's failure statistics means 10 million of our 28 million businesses are heading towards failure right now.

There are standing failures, too, like businesses going but ownership not getting paid. Some are successful businesses but failed owners losing relationships, spouses, health, faith, free time and enjoyment of life. Things can go wrong and *Small Business Survival 101* identifies them.

Did you know only one company, GE, is left from the original Dow 100? There are only 202 Fortune 500 companies from 1982 still standing. Starting a business is clearly easier than staying in business whether the business is big or small. Perhaps only a fatal illness damages as much as a failed business. People lose jobs, owners lose wealth, credit, self esteem and maybe health and marriage. Vendors get left on the hook. Maybe there are lawsuits.

I wrote this book to help you avoid all that.

Small businesses are touted as job creators and innovators. True, but how much does this continual carnage erase the gain? Most of it. Small businesses lose about as many jobs as they create. In 2010 some 400,000 small businesses closed. In 2010 there were 394,000 start ups according to the Kauffman foundation. Employment by small businesses has remained at a significant 50% of the workforce. There are more businesses than there is business. Truth be told, our need is not as great for starting new businesses as it is keeping those in business already up. The present fragmented system of training entrepreneurs, if that is what it can be called, is a monumental failure and signals widespread irresponsibility.

I am certain business owners are immediately drawn to the serious subject matter of *Small Business Survival 101*. I am just as certain that only a business owner can credibly write it. Too much business writing is academia or milquetoast lists of dos and don'ts and not lived experience of a tenured owner. There are no sacred cows and I even skewer a few. *Small Business Survival 101* shows you the best businesses to be in for the long term. It presents a no-nonsense picture of who you need to be to operate such a business.

The bottom line is that most failures occur from owner incompetence and slack preparation. As proud and determined as he can be, a business owner is often his own worst enemy by not seeking the advice needed or by operating on inadequate skills. The right guidance is crucial and *Small Business Survival 101* contains it. Every page has nuggets of business protein to nourish a business. I hope you find *Small Business Survival 101* a treatise on lasting entrepreneurship.

This book is written for forming businesses and those formed but lacking longevity elements. These eight chapters will increase the soundness of your business.

The most lovable thing about business owners is sometimes they do not know what they don't know. They are in love with what they do even as an iceberg approaches. Epiphanies go a long way here and *Small Business Survival 101* provides them. There is a Yiddish saying, "It ends as it begins." Too many entrepreneurs begin unschooled and fail similarly so I hope to provide some schooling.

Small Business Survival 101 details, in poignant language, experiences from mild to harrowing, to wonderful, of owning my businesses. They provide decades of 20/20 hindsight. Further credentials include gray hair and meeting 768 straight payrolls without a bounced check. I have published 102 columns as *The Small Business Advisor* so if I haven't lived it, I've seen it.

Small Business Survival 101 distills the pillars of longevity to eight. Why eight? Because that's all there are. You may hear others expressed but they will still come under one of these eight. *Small Business Survival 101* takes aim at existing platitudes and debunks some. But knowing something is easy and executing it is harder so learn how with this book.

There is new vocabulary. Understand "Going Out Of Business By Design" and "Deciding While Intoxicated." Owners will be instructed to "Not Get Behind On Their Competence." Readers learn the "Law of The Pinball" and to avoid "Mona Lisas." "Winning Ugly" methods are here if needed. You will see the importance of selling products that "Eat and Drink" and the differences between "Wantapreneurs, Solopreneurs and Salepreneurs." There are sections on "Sales Menopause" and the very important "Know Your Numbers." I probe the entrepreneur's mind with "The Owner's Eye" and "The Mind of an Owner." The same is done with the salesperson's brain which can be difficult to find words for. The most effective leadership method taught is to "Treat Everyone Differently."

Most business literature is about starting a business. There is not enough about staying in business. *Small Business Survival 101* is a comprehensive book about staying up. *Small Business Survival 101* is not a collection of funny stories or greatest hits. It is useful methodology and pierced mythology gleaned from trench warfare. Lessons come from dogs, hobbies, employees, my wife, my lawyer, mentors, troubles, my bathroom countertop, financial statements, competitors, customers, vendors and bankers—all who give lessons from live combat, the best kind. There may be views some disagree with but they are my views gleaned from living the sometimes dreamy life of owning your own business.

Owning a business is a marriage for the distance. And many make it. I have. If you are a business owner between the formative state and the magical seven year mark then you benefit the most from *Small Business Survival 101* principles. *Small Business Survival 101* makes you think and shows where to change. Most of the principles can be implemented in short order. Some can be good reading for the entrepreneurial-thinking manager driving any profit center.

There is no finish line in business. You are never there but must always have eyes on the threats and strategies to deflect them. That is what I show you in this book.

Let's get to it!

Tom Pease
tcivlj@aol.com
901-484-0105

1

Touring Entrepreneur Land And Meriting Citizenship

T o reach full entrepreneurship requires weapons-grade expertise from you. Would you hire you for such a mission? This chapter takes a hard look at what is needed of you for this role, where your 'preneur path should lead, who you need to be to get there, and visits critical formative decisions start-ups make. *Small Business Survival 101* shows you how to put expertise to use to build a business that lasts and how to progress to your entrepreneurship sweet spot.

I mentioned I like the Yiddish saying "It begins as it ends". This chapter guides you to beginning right so that you end right—whatever that means for you—but I suggest it means staying in business. These principles not only apply to newly forming businesses but also those seeking expansion or diversification. Both of those processes are similar to forming new businesses that seek longevity.

There are two basic avenues to establishing your own business. One is the I-Have-An-Idea approach and the other is the Serve-An-

Apprenticeship method. The former is really not a model but an irrational passion for your idea and that is about all you have. You hope to sell it to investors, hit it big and soon, or flip it for cash. It is usually not a long term strategy and budding business people in this category have limited expertise and act like it. The strength of the model is the idea itself. The second method, far more successful, approaches entrepreneurship as a profession and prepares accordingly. The strength of this plan resides in the owner's expertise. This means having the experience, having the business education and soloing at the right time. This method is used by most lasting entrepreneurs although the Idea Method gets the headlines. We probe the two models but present apprenticeship as the way to go for longevity.

In either case their success depends upon *you*.

Whichever method you use it is only a passport to entry and by no means enough to gain permanent residency. Let's look at how that is done.

Doctors go to medical school before hanging shingles proclaiming M.D. Lawyers go to law school and pilots to flight school. Electricians study under a master electrician before certification so not to electrocute anyone. Accountants pass a CPA exam before advising on taxes. Soldiers must complete boot camp before soldiering. Even hairdressers go to beauty school and must pass tests before licensed to cut hair publicly. Engineers spend five years learning to build things that do not collapse and kill people. These professionals have low failure rates, can give advice, perform services and charge for them because they have the bona fides for what they claim to be. They have it to give. You cannot give what you do not have!

Credentials answer customers' questions of "Do you have it?" and "Are you real?" They garner the credibility that produces customer expectations of good results and get you business. If formed and forming entrepreneurs would follow the example of these professionals there would be fewer failures. What do many wantapreneurs do to prepare for their profession? Too often the answer is "not much."

Here is the question concerning your role as president: would you consider yourself qualified if you were hiring YOU for the job?

In high school I was on the wrestling team. The football coach was the wrestling coach and did not know much wrestling but he was still called the coach. He kept us focused and in shape but we lost many matches because he was not a real wrestling coach, not expert. The next year we hired a recent collegiate wrestler as coach. He knew all the moves and what it took because he was a collegiate wrestler. In two years the same rag tags were state champions because of the considerable expertise this coach had to give which became the difference between our success and failure. We were a success because of his expertise. It was transformative because it was real. Both called themselves wrestling coaches but only one had it to give us and he did.

Wantapreneurs frequently do not have it to give to customers, employees, or their business, because there are no certifications to be an entrepreneur. None. Thus, the budding can be short on the necessary bona fides, winging it, learning on the job and trying to compete against those with the goods. In would not be uncommon that wantapreneurs represent themselves as competent, or at least think they are, in things they aren't. The top reason cited for business failures is mismanagement, a broad way of saying owner incompetence or that you don't have it. There are about 28 million small businesses, some 9,000 in my city counting solopreneurs, so it is not likely any marketplace does not already have the expertise. That is the ocean you enter to make your waves stand out.

Only you can make yourself a successful owner. Success comes from knowing what you are doing and from a business model that can last. It will not come from less meaty things like people feeding your ego or the quote of the day or getting some funding. Help yourself by getting all training first! Ben Franklin: "An investment in education pays the best dividend." Amen.

There are plenty of so-called business owners that fail becoming statistics from working flimsy plans with not enough bearing on the reality of their skills. Take an honest inventory of yourself. There are leadership methods to learn, numbers to understand, strategies to use, ratios to calculate, financials to interpret, customers to win, sales to be made, problems to solve, and changes to deal with. Learn these because our competitive markets won't reward, unprepared and, yes, unqualified business owners. It simply spits them out. Economist Herb Stein said it: "What cannot go on won't."

Start-up strategy is not just for start-ups, either. Established businesses looking to expand or diversify by taking on a new product or geography go through similar processes.

Opening a business without the needed expertise is walking the plank no matter how strong the encouragement, but it goes on frequently. Work on weaknesses before you open to reduce failures. Unfortunately, as I said, there are no requirements to certify business competency, which contributes to the lack of it, and tempts neophytes to dive in before its time. You can get a tax number, pay a fee for a license and declare yourself president of a company. But this makes you only a wantapreneur or maybe somebody snorting business cocaine. It is as nonsensical as saying, "I am hopping this plane I've never flown and fly my family to Disneyland."

Crazy, crazy.

Perhaps it is all because of the mental state, understandable as it is, of striving entrepreneurs summarized by John Greenleaf Whittier in *Maud Muller*: "For all the sad words of tongue or pen, the saddest are these: It might have been." Our strivers don't want this to be said of them nor leave anything on the table, both admirable ambitions in the pursuit of any goal.

Entrepreneurs, and I use this word for those that deserve it meaning those having a functioning business, must know more than many professionals to be successful. Yet, again, nothing is required. Many are winging it. Maybe winging it with flair. Maybe winging it and not looking like you are, but still winging it. This does not work any better for forming a business than a high-schooler trying to pass the PhD. A business license ought to license competence but it only shows you paid a fee. Maybe this ease-of-entry is free enterprise at is best but it can be a path to a nightmare. Licensing requirements demonstrating expertise in accounting, marketing, contracting, employing, leading, selling and financing would reduce failures.

My wife is a mental health counselor (thank goodness for me) and must pass in-service training courses yearly to renew her license since she deals with the serious matter of mental health. Having the right to operate a business should have educational requirements for everyone's well being too.

The scandalously high failure statistics, which damage the economy, landlords, creditors, capital, jobs, accounts receivable and just self-esteem, cry out for more preparation, which is what apprenticing provides. Only three industries guarantee a future: French fries, toilet paper, and women's cosmetics. The rest fight it out! Take heart that you will likely be an overnight success but that 365 other nights will precede that day. There may also be nightmares.

Can you interpret a financial statement? Can you distinguish between cash flow and profit? Can you compute your current ratio? Do you know how many times you turn inventory? Are you keeping an AR aging? Are you aware of the many taxes that have nothing to do with profit? Do you know what it takes to borrow money? Can you lead? Can you sell? Are you fit? Those are just a few primer questions for you.

"You can't give what you don't have."

Let's begin this with a brain check. Let's ensure we are reading ourselves correctly, as well as business conditions and political climate. These three spheres influence our thoughts, actions, decisions, and attitudes and we don't want mis-reads yielding us erroneous dispositions. We want to be as smart as possible and avoid doing stupid stuff.

To be a good golfer, shoot your lowest scores and win you need a complete set of clubs to conquer the course. If you knowingly leave putter and driver at the clubhouse and head out to play anyway you would be just plain stupid. If you left them and did not know you were then that would be carelessness. No matter which reason either results in you not playing your best and that is on you. There are too many entrepreneurs playing without a full set either which is why they fail. We can learn something from Abe Lincoln about preparedness when he said: "If I am going to spend six hours cutting down a tree I spend the first two sharpening my ax." You will get a description of the business clubs needed to survive and prosper by reading this book, which will make you smarter. If you won't do them then you are increasing failure chances.

The margin for error in small business is small and you can reduce that margin by staying spec'd up in your industry. To not do so, to run on emotion, to not be up to speed, to live in denial or listen to the wrong people, is being stupid. Being stupid costs money, maybe all you have.

Owing a business is a fairly serious matter and the failures show more straight talk about why this happens is needed which is what we do in this book. Sometimes when I do that people may say I am being negative. I do not much worry about triggering emotions as long as I am being *accurate.*

Let's be smart about interpreting conditions small businesses find themselves in today and suggest their right view. The Great Recession has been an economic Viet Nam and downsized the whole economy. A chunk of buying power left the building. The game is now hardball and softball is no longer played. But this has been going on for years and should be factored in by now. It could be the New Normal but it is where we have been, meaning its effect is now diluted. This climate has produced certain invalid excuse making by some.

You hear " if government quits strangling small business with regulations and red tape they could prosper." That just does not go on in most small businesses. If an owner sets out to make ten sales calls or a company conducts a marketing blitz there is no government agent tailing him with forms or issuing a citation for failure to make a sale. There are enough pro small business government programs like loans, tax holidays, first year write offs, time payment for taxes, various bankruptcy chapters, that help a small business. Remember too, there are not even regulations to meet to start a business so that could not be less restrictive.

Get Smart

There really can be no excuse-making for a small business owner's lack of understanding of business essentials anyway. Excuses make you feel better but won't make the business better. Getting smart will. For example, if a loan is declined it is because you didn't deserve one and must improve your understanding of creditworthiness and interpreting your financial blood work. If you get beat up by the competition that is too bad because competition is our way. You have to become the competition that the competition complains about. If you think you are hurt because you are a minority think again. The marketplace does not care. The point is it just all depends upon YOU. It depends upon how smart you are and about how much smarter you can be.

Ann Landers liked to say "Fifty per cent of doctors are in the bottom half of their class." This is true of entrepreneurs, too. There are business owners in the top 10% and those in the bottom 10%. Increase your business intelligence by improving competency in your field. You can't give your business what you don't have. Make it your mission to get what's missing. Your future depends upon it. Remember what my wrestling coach gave our team because that is the same stuff you want to give your business if you want it to win.

To get smart about operating a small business or entrepreneurship is not easy. There are not actual curriculums and you get most of that from years attending Setback University. In college you can cobble together courses in accounting, marketing, salesmanship, management, and finance. That gets you book knowledge but you won't see needed courses like "Working Your Ass Off" or "Getting The Most From The Least" or "Containing Fear, Uncertainty and Doubt" or "Creating Positive Cash Flow". To get actual experience intern at a small business and ask the owner to show you the business's inner workings and share his thoughts as he handles the good, the bad and the ugly. That may be the best education.

Educators themselves need better education or the teaching requirements and barring anyone without a Masters degree from teaching should be changed. I have 32 years running my business but cannot be faculty because I lack the Masters. Yet, someone who has never worked could get his bachelor degree, then an MBA, and teach business without ever working in one. This does not make much sense nor is it smart. The lack of business teachers who owned businesses gives rise to self-appointed business gurus, some close to imposters. Non-profit and quasi-government groups put the mantle on to teach entrepreneurship. But what non-profit should teach profit? It is not hard to see why small business failures are so high.

Serve An Apprenticeship

Since there are no requirements to begin a business the smart thing is acting like there are courses to master and requirements to meet. Start by apprenticing where you work. What you do now is hopefully similar to your entrepreneurial plans. Observe the marketing guy, the finance guy, the production manager and the boss. Ask questions. Note marketing strategies and tactics that work and those that don't. Go to seminars if your company will send you. Stretch yourself with work in another department to see how it suits you and what you can learn. Audit appropriate classes at your university. Find a mentor entrepreneur who will save the superficial rah rah and answer hard questions honestly.

Business ownership is best worked into intelligently as an apprenticeship until the experience is there. At a minimum, have the professional expertise, courses in accounting and marketing, and know sales to eliminate these failure factors. Opening your own deal means you start at the top as CEO even if it is just you and a few. To my knowledge, there is no such position as a CEO trainee. CEO's are expected to know business and what they are doing which takes education and experience, not just ideas they are crazy about. You are expected to know the best processes, to be expert in what your business does, how to manage it and how to grow it.

I apprenticed by selling office equipment for five years. I called on large accounts and small ones. I lost accounts and gained accounts. I had good months and bad. I learned to compete. I experienced the uncertainty common to salespeople known as FUD-Fear, Uncertainty and Doubt, and I learned to deal with it. I went to sales schools. All of this was great training for going on my own. I had enough industry knowledge and sales experience to make a good start.

Know something about every business function because you will have employees. How will you know they are doing the job if you do not know their job? If employees perceive you are lacking you will lose respect needed to lead. This is like expecting a quarterback to be successful without knowing the plays. A National Car Rental advertisement has a great one-liner about this: "*Your core competency is competency.*" I love this line. It so gets to my point and could well be a chapter title.

An attraction of entrepreneurship is that you get market rates if you possess the competency. You may have worked as an apprentice electrician, accountant, salesperson, technician, or law clerk for, say, $30 an hour but on your own the market may be $100 an hour or more. Sounds like a big raise! Well, sure, providing you get enough work. Once you realize the cost of overhead and acquiring customers you feel it's never enough.

Lawyers charge $225 an hour. Counselors are $75 an hour. A psychiatrist gets $300. A network technician can be $125 an hour. The tow truck guy may be $400 an hour to extract you. Experts in any field make good money because they are experts. Joke about this: A doctor threw a party and the toilet clogged. A plumber came and fixed it in short order. He presented his $195 bill to the doctor. The doc exclaimed "$195 for half an hour's work. I am a doctor and I don't get that kind of money. "I know," said the plumber. "I had the same problem when I was a doctor."

Be An Expert In Something
Business ownership is a difficult place for on the job training because the clock is always ticking but too often it is where upstarts learn

which contributes to failure. Already be that industry expert out of the gate, from apprenticing, to reduce fatal errors. Make sure those hired are expert, too, if you want a company expert in what it does. A small business is only as good as its people so don't scrimp here. It will be false economy. Hopefully these employees have served apprenticeships too. You get what you pay for; especially when it comes to those paid to relate to customers like sales and technical people. These are the ones bringing in the money and establishing relationships. Saving a few dollars here ends up costing you many later. Most successful owners hire the best person they can find which decreases failures. If you will not put in the time to hire right then the consequences are on you.

Failure rates are rising because owning a business is appealing with the workplace uncertainty. But starting one as a default choice is a poor choice. This necessity of a sort does the prospective owner no favors unless schooled for this mission. Too much 'going into business for myself' is a fool's errand because the owner is not yet expert. Many traveling this road end up effectively as an outside salesperson for themselves, a one-man-band selling a skill to earn a living. They have created a job, own a job, and not a business.

Might you be better off as an outside salesperson for an established company and work on commission? At least you have support, training and someone else's working capital and the same shot at making money. Or, this could serve as the apprenticeship you need. Just about any business would hire an outside sales person on straight commission, which is great training and advisable experience *before* you open. It is an environment much like starting a business.

All that said, an unspoken truth about entrepreneurs is they cannot work for anyone or with anyone. They are too independent, have personalities that do not mesh, will not obtain the skills to be employed, do not like supervising others, have poor health habits, or other psychological factors making them unemployable. If so, then being a solopreneur, or you and a few, may be the best opportunity for fulfillment.

Over 70% of small businesses are categorized as solopreneurships. I have a hard time recognizing solopreneurships as 'real businesses'. There are no employees to manage so no people management skills are needed. You can't gain market share with just one person. The solopreneur owns a job and not a company, if they even own that, and never growing beyond one person means you may not be that great an employee either. That is not to say solos do not have a good living or are not great businesspeople. I say they just don't yet own a business. Data shows that 6 million of the 28 million small businesses have paid employees. This means the remainder are supporting one person, the owner, or not even doing that.

Your Time Has Come?

There is a time to become your boss and a time to wait. As mentioned, a primary reason businesses fail is owners do not yet have the necessary acumen. The only way to get it is experience, which takes time. Take the time. For a tree trunk to show a growth ring it must grow a year. It can't show one in three months and neither can you.

In college I was an IBM sales assistant, an errand boy. The manager asked me to take a portable dictation unit and canvass a building to sample sales work. I was 19. I took the hand unit and brochures into the high rise and quickly took a seat in the lobby and a few deep breathes. I did not want to do this and really did not know what I was doing although I could demonstrate the unit. It was a great job as a student, I wanted to impress so I gutted out going into every office on every floor. It took days. I only got to a real decision maker twice that wanted a demonstration. (I related this to a senior class in entrepreneurship at the University of Memphis, thinking it apropos, which it was, but a big laugh broke hearing 'dictation unit').

I did a decent job with those two prospects and handed that information to the sales guy who closed one. The manager praised me and wanted to talk. I was clear: " I never want to do that no matter what the pay." I returned to well-paid errand boy while finishing college not knowing valuable experience had stored to my hard drive.

I spent two years in the Navy and then had a few jobs when my father in law asks about interviewing at IBM because he knew the manager. At the time I was selling and writing commercials. I had to laugh but said sure. I was married and 25. The branch manager was intrigued by my IBM experience.

I said I never saw myself as a salesperson. "What are you doing now?" he asked. "I write commercials and hope they buy air time with my ideas," I answered. "You are a salesperson," he said. I hired on at what seemed like a lot of pay. I spent two months in the branch and one in Dallas in a sales dormitory for extensive training. I didn't like it. In Dallas I awoke each morning with a stomach ache if I did sleep. I called my wife half way and said this was not for me and I was quitting. She said to calm down and came to discuss. That helped and I talked with the instructor saying I felt I did not belong because they never seemed to like what I was doing, always criticized me, and I would drop out if not for my wife.

I was just scared and not very sure of myself. "Tom, we understand. We are sorry it hit you like that but there is pressure in sales work and we build that in. We normally don't do this but we think you are among our strongest candidates." Well, knock me over with a feather. It took all that just to stay the month. Others had the same difficulty. In any case, the first six months of any new salesperson's life, just like a business owner's, are a combination of excitement, fear and plenty of doubt.

Fast forward five years and I am salesperson of the year twice out of 21 good reps, and once 19th in the country of 4000 making great money and happy. I could not believe how I took to the work, was good at it, and loved it, but this is not a greatest hits tour. There is a tremendously important business lesson here, which is DON'T GO UNTIL READY. Ownership is too demanding to wing it. The good news is you may not be ready now but can be later. Significant failures are caused by the "too soon" syndrome, not dissimilar from other too soon decisions like marrying too soon, going pro too soon, selling stock too soon or starting through an intersection too soon. As we saw, in college I was not ready for sales work. Six years more of life experience and I was. It prepared me to do it without me really knowing that. Experience is everything. Leave base early and you are thrown out! How many high school athletes successfully go straight to MLB or the NFL? How many medical students perform appendectomies? Is your child ready for the 8th grade right out of 5th grade? Let's borrow from the Boy Scouts: Be Prepared!

This is about ownership and so far I am just successful at office equipment sales but expert at it. Six years into sales I am craving independence from big corporate. I wanted my own thing, even for less money. That was my passion, independence. Still is. I am prickly and don't like anyone telling me what to do. I only am qualified for that and would not make a good employee. Sound like you? I am 31 and seeking self boss-hood so I can work for someone as smart as myself. I lacked knowledge concerning business operations though. I didn't know payroll taxes, FUTA, SUTA, FICA, workman's comp, inventory turns, hurdle rate, current ratio, gross margin, net present value, and the rest.

I never heard of them yet these are the DNA of a business. Neither did my partners who were "business people". There were three of us starting with me as sales guy. I did well ringing $500,000 the first year so was shocked when we received notice they were padlocking us since we hadn't paid certain taxes in six months. One partner supposedly knew that stuff but didn't. We sold everything to raise that and then had no cash. Brother. We were bit big because we were stupid on important things and still learning the hard, expensive way. Somebody needed experience in accounting. Shortly after that one partner wanted to sell his part, which I bought, making me majority owner.

You're Never There

From experience I learned what I didn't know *after a few years*. Selling copiously forgives sins and I was in the super salesman category, which forgave blunders and bought priceless time until we functioned as a real business. Don't go off half-cocked with scant business experience juiced on excitement. It won't get you there. Do not go, either, without understanding the pressures (see below). Keep that excitement while learning, though, and get the education. NOW you are positioned to succeed and not wreck lives. Get further education from trade associations like real estate associations, computer reseller associations, or merchants associations. They all sponsor seminars, in person and online, to keep members current. Trade associations are vital for continuing ed and networking with others like you.

It is instructive to think of your business as a practice instead of a corporation, like doctors and attorneys. They are called such because the dynamics frequently change and new knowledge enters the profession that must be assimilated just like in business. These professionals feel they are never 'there' thus are practicing their craft. It will be likewise for you. You are never there, either, and are practicing business always.

It should be obvious to stick with what you know. What you know and have done provides evidence of what you like to do, can do, and have expertise in. Don't spend years in computer networking and then open a restaurant—a waste of experience. Let's summarize: know your craft and stick with what you know, and stay in the know. "The owner must know!"

Know Your Predominant Trait

Crucial to your success, and your employees' too, is knowing your predominant trait. There is a dominant personality trait that controls and you build your business around it. If a detail person you would not like creative work. If a creative person you won't like parameters. An independence freak will not do well with partners. Make sure you read the trait correctly. It is like buying a vehicle. If you have a large family a van is the predominant choice. If a single male it's a sports car baby. If an outdoorsman then a four-wheel drive predominates. All three are cars but distinguished by their predominant trait.

Here is a story about this. There is a very good golfer who plays extensively. He plays tournaments, scrambles and dogfights. He travels to other courses. He plays 36 holes a day. He is on the practice tee a lot. He has a coach. He golfs, golfs, golfs and loves golf. He decides it is his life and buys a golf course to live his passion. But most of the time he is busy growing grass, mowing grass, dealing with weather, repairing plumbing, watering, keeping sand in the traps, hiring workers, organizing events, buying golf carts, stocking the pro shop, meeting a payroll and rarely playing golf. He was not happy. He did not have passion for operations but that is what was called for. Too late he realized his passion was *playing* golf, not *managing* golf, and he would be happier trying to become golf pro. Know yourself.

There are a few traits that might disqualify you for business ownership. If you are a control freak, orderly, fold your tee shirts, and like to live organized, business ownership might be torture. A business, largely controlled by customers and not you, frequently resembles a teenager's closet. If you are the uncompetitive type, preferring everyone get a trophy, you will not do well. If you are not physically fit that hurts because the state of mind follows the body and you need all your wits in this gig. If you have ADHD, this could be a blessing or a curse. I have some and it keeps more gas in the tank than most people and puts forth a turbo charged effort when needed. If it turns you into a scatter brain then this is not good. Some say 'right brain' people succeed in business more than 'left brain' or vice versa. I can tell you that to succeed in business long term you need a whole brain.

You're Passionate

A non-negotiable trait is passion—weapons grade—the power that overcomes obstacles and doubt mere mortals cannot. It is rocket fuel that puts you into orbit and keeps you there. It is one of the top "haves" to succeed. You know real passion what you felt when you chased your future spouse, tried to lower your golf score or catch bigger fish. This passion is a form of temporary insanity and thank goodness since there are insane challenges to overcome that could not be without this equal force of insanity opposing them!

When I started Kawasaki of Memphis, for example, I was reporting to my office equipment company regularly wearing a suit and directing traffic. I was earning a good living but bored and running low on passion. Imagine then, chasing a 1.3 million dollar SBA loan to build a

12,000 square foot building on a corner lot to make something out of a grass field. What makes one do this is the temporary insanity passion and in my case for motorcycles. I pictured my gleaming showroom full of gorgeous two-wheeled road rockets people love to ride including me.

We opened and I spent two years tirelessly working the showroom selling motorcycles and ATVs, even as still responsible for my 25 employee office equipment company. I would never have done this as a regular job but here I was irrationally waiting on customers, completing credit apps, and closing deals with relish because of my passion for the success of the mission. It was this passion that overcame any barrier. We got it together and after two years I quit the floor but it was a critical two years helping to make money and garner market information from customers.

Passion goes through periods. Start up requires that enjoyable temporary insanity. Next comes team building as you assemble the parts. After accomplishing the team building establish a competent operating unit that allows you to exit the insanity mode *altogether* into enjoyment mode, the so-called working-on-the-business-and not- in-it mode. Do enjoy that temporary insanity start up mode; it may be the best one. Do exit operating mode one day or you may become permanently insane. I love the answer given by Muhtar Kent, CEO of Coke, when asked about how long he wanted to do what he was doing: "It just depends on how long I get the psychic income," he said. Well said, in one sentence, as to what moves entrepreneurs as much as money. Psychic income ... let's borrow that cool term and equate it with passion.

Understand The Pressures

One reason pressure bears on a business owner is he does not pay attention to the broader ramifications he sets in motion. Once a business begins expectations are created. Picture the business day one. It is just you at center court. You hire a few employees and they have expectations. Soon customers arrive with needs. Families have interests in the business's well being so they come. Bankers and insurers have expectations so they attend. Your landlord is there. Vendors are watching, some with performance expectations and payment demands. Tax collecting agents watch and want to collect. Hopefully more customers arrive which brings more expectations. You have to deliver or may be heckled, booed, or yes, cheered!

You did want to own a business, right? These expectations are part of it and keep coming. "I want more liquidity in your financials!" exhorts the banker. "Sales need to increase!" shouts your manufacturer. "I need a raise!" demands an employee. Customers may say "How come you take so long?" Suppliers yell "where is payment?" You may feel like the mole in the Whack-A-Mole game. It is just the nature of it. Don't forget that competitors arrive to play against you and plant doubt. You can't call time out either. These pressures follow you always. Are we there yet? Never.

The start of each month may find you feeling you fell on a few hand grenades. But, by its end, you may have closed enough business to feel you relegated Bill Gates to a speck in your rear view mirror. Can you live like this? Hope so. It would be a good sign if you enjoy roller coasters. Of course you do, because their ride is *exciting* as will be riding your business ups and downs.

Be one competitive, knowledgeable, fit, smart, creative, passionate, multi tasking, problem-solving leader to win in this environment and love it. You have to thrive on this controlled chaos. Understand this because you are in command and captains are not formed sailing still waters. I have done this for three decades and know! The degree of difficulty is comparable to learning to fly, say, a multi engine with instrument flight rating. This has a higher qualification than learning to drive. It's not most people can't be trained to fly but they have to train, put in the time, or crash taking everyone with them just like crashing a business.

The Incomplete Truth

Entrepreneurs get nuked because they don't possess the complete truth but rather an incomplete version leaving off reality. The first encounter: "I am going for it. I always wanted my own business. I have this killer idea. I admire Donald Trump. I have always loved...... fill in the blank. I like being my own boss." Familiar thoughts but here is the lost sentence: " I really do not have a professional picture of what it takes to run a business and have no experience doing so but people have really encouraged me about my idea." Which is why failures are high.

Next, the upstart gets money and goes into start-up-itis. "We must have Macs, space to make us look good, brochures, knock out website, wrap out cars, logo designed, letterhead of a quality, picture business cards, Smart Board, great furniture, buy ads in church bulletins, join the BBB, Chamber, and possibly the YMCA. We need to get the word out." Phase this stuff in and don't do it all at once. It burns precious time and working capital. The left off sentence: "Whew. We blew through serious cash to look good but still don't have customers." It's like using lipstick to make the pig into a princess or trying to get an upgrade on the Titanic. Let your business look good on its own as well as float in its own water before you start decorating.

How much is hollow posturing to look the part before you are the part? Finish the window dressing *after* you have a following of customers and conserve precious cash. Actually, it is wisest to stay in frugal start up mode! Moving along, you have exciting months. The intoxicated CEO tells himself this is surely the beginning and commits to even more as if it will always be such. It won't! It could be the high point for a while. I opened the Kawasaki dealership and the newness drew a crowd. We sold 45 bikes our third month but took two years to do that again. The reality sentence: "We had a few encouraging months but should not increase overhead until sustained revenue rises."

Do You Fit The Definition?

Idea wantapreneurs usually lack needed expertise but feel they do not need it because they possess an idea they are passionate about. This is common. They have something novel, perhaps, and are plenty excited. Their overuse of unearned hyperbolic words, especially 'great', are thrown around. Others stir them, encourage them to start a business, and become convinced their idea is the next big thing or at least something.

They search for investors to pay them to play with their idea. It is likely there is little revenue. These are businesses the way ketchup is a vegetable and can't swim without water wings. They are armed with a butter knife and a napkin. These upstarts enjoy pulling out Christmas decorations before the tree is up. Paaaleeeeeese have the business acumen to know what to do with your idea before you romance it. If not, maybe you could be fortunate to hire someone who does.

To support my point visit Etsy.com. It has thousands of innovative products for sale by craftsmen with novel ideas. Yet, most languish, selling some, yes, but not into a real business. Then remember the person with the Pet Rock. He sold plenty. Would that be because of the overwhelming genius of the idea? No. It was pretty useless. But it was due to the overwhelming skill of that rock entrepreneur who knew a lot about business. Its success was not due to the strength of the idea but to the strength of the business person.

There are no shortages of good ideas but are shortages of ideas that make real businesses. There are serious shortages of people who can make an idea a business. You may have one or ten ideas by next week but this does not make you an entrepreneur or mean any idea is a business. I do not mean to be bashing ideas. The word entrepreneur is closely identified with ideas which is as it should be. There is great demand for ideas in business. Their main need is in *running* a business. Good ideas are constantly needed to motivate employees, to win customers, to market yourself, to land good employees, to solve problems, to deal with change, to enter new markets, to maintain profitability and on and on. You may need 5,000 ideas in an entire career just to accomplish these!

As you hawk around your idea have at least $100,000 annual gross profit, per principle, to deserve respect and prove your idea is not a hobby. Otherwise you are little more than a carnival barker. Again, the shortages are in finding people that make businesses from ideas and if trying to slough off this proof-of-idea work find something else to play with. I was once discussing the high failure statistics with a business broker who commented: "Yeah they are high but not that high for real businesspeople." Exactly, and you are not one of those at this point.

Let us take a moment and summarize what we need so far to succeed: a) a great idea we are passionate about b) the idea improves a product or process known to be needed/wanted c) strong expertise in your industry AND in the business of business and d) personality traits compatible with the business.

Shark Tank Lessons

Catch *Shark Tank* for real lessons in entrepreneurship from real business people. These five sharks, accomplished centa-millionaires, listen to pitches from entrepreneurs, hyped as they are, but will not touch them if no record of sales no matter what the idea. They do not fund ideas without portfolio. Investors are looking for something already going, something to actually invest in. The Sharks say, in addition to sales, they want to see unbridled passion and commitment. If you have seen this show, which is fantastic, you see those with great ideas and then those with great ideas *and* a sales track. If you appear on Shark Tank with a pretty cool idea, but no sales to speak of, here is what the Sharks will offer you: NOTHING.

What you do not see by these pitchers sometimes is common sense. Often the candidates tell these centa-millionaire sharks they will "not take less than" such and such—sort of like God welcoming you into the kingdom but you negotiate your mansion and end up tossed. If you are ever fortunate enough to negotiate with accomplished people it is not their money that makes your success but their connections. If Mark Cuban offers you something you say not only yes, but hell yes, because you want his *venture connections* more than his venture capital. Shark Tank follow ups find upstarts doubling or tripling business within a year because the sharks can pick up the phone and get a product national distribution. They have the keys to the country. Let that be a lesson— seek venture connections more than venture capital.

Too Many Mona Lisas

If you are only excited about an idea, and not operating a business, building a business, sustaining a business, and enjoying that whole idea—RED FLAG. It is the equivalent of wanting to paint, awesome scenes in mind, but not liking the part about brushes and colors. It is wanting to be a doctor without med school. *It is a business first and an idea second.* You go into business, not into idea, and just because you have an idea you love does not grant you some inalienable right to business ownership. Businesses only about ideas, and not the business of business, I call Mona Lisas because they look best on paper or in the eye of the beholder. It is the business person who makes the idea and it is not the idea that makes the business person.

To this point I will describe an event in Memphis put on, to great fanfare, for start-up entrepreneurs, by Nibletz.com. Nibletz presents itself as a national presence and "The Voice of Startups Everywhere Else". The event was to help upstarts "explore entrepreneurial ecosystems" whatever that means. There was great fanfare and 2,000 bought tickets for the week's programs. After it was over Nibletz left $60,000 in unpaid bills from the conference. Its president consequently resigned and was asked what happened. His incredible response: "I am bad at handling business." This from the head of a company purporting to teach business. Amazing, really, but this lack of credentials is not uncommon. Things like this recall dot.com bust stuff.

Entrepreneurs should ask periodically "What am I really doing and why am I doing it? Am I doing things for the right reason? Am I actually doing business?" There are many wrong answers but one right one: "I have passion for owning a business so I can pursue my advocacy passion to which I am well suited." Yes, it takes two distinct passions. Let's check the dictionary here: "Entrepreneur—one who organizes, manages, finances and assumes the responsibility of a business." I would add that it supports the owner. Educators in entrepreneurship should keep this definition in sight along with this subheading: "YOU have to do it."

Too many today are mis-using the term entrepreneur, really aren't one, but do fit wantapreneur. Upstarts today have other ideas of our definition, or lost sight of it, but it has not changed. Zero money wantapreneurs don a tee shirt, spit buzz words, get a laptop/ smart phone, and point to something they developed to be considered wonderful even though it has little business-wise to back this up like revenue, employees and working capital. Their concept more closely resembles a science project. By all means press on but realize where you are and where you aren't.

Entrepreneur Career Path
Apprenticeship > Wantapreneur > Salepreneur > Solopreneur >
Entrepreneur > Intrapreneur
"Entrepreneuress" describes a female entrepreneur.
Virtualpreneur: works in the cloud

To be an entrepreneur means you get it done on your own. You do it. That is the nature of the beast and if you cannot, and there are too many who can't, chose another profession. You just have to have the talent to do this. It can't be faked, outsourced or gifted. This hard-to-define can do ability cannot be taught. It is doubtful you could instruct Babe Ruth into being a home run king or Usain Bolt into world's fastest human. They just have something. You can throw money at a wannabe but that won't make him a gonnabe. As you will hear me repeat, you get a much better return if you throw expertise at it. In entrepreneurship, nobody owes you nor are you entitled to anything. You earn it. That is why successful entrepreneurs are admired—because they do Frank Sinatra—they do it their way. These are the 30% that survive long term.

Incubator Model Needs an Upgrade

It is trendy for cities to have incubators renting space to budding entrepreneurs, sometimes for a specific industry, and teaching some basics. It is more or less a business frat house. Some tenants do not incubate out and become permanent residents. Incubators may actually encourage in the wrong direction, though, by rustling up people with ideas but little else, like working capital, and trying to force business success.

These entities are non-profits existing on grants and run by non business owners. How is that a success model for aspiring newbies? Their subsidized financing says incubators can't stand on their merits which is what entrepreneurship is about. Incubators' track record for establishing lasting start-ups, their purpose for being, is not good and you do not hear much about their long term hatchlings. I am not saying there aren't any, there are, they are just miniscule in number for all the hoopla, especially compared to other start-ups that do not use an incubator which is the great majority. In Memphis a recent group of twelve who went through the boot camps, and all the rest, progressed to Investor's Day where pitches were given seeking funding. None got an offer. Instead of all the incubating leading to an Investor Day it should culminate in a "Now Work Your Ass Off Day" where you actually begin to be a business person, deserve the title entrepreneur, and sell your product which raises its own money.

If the existing presentation of entrepreneurship, that being just come up with a good idea, go through an incubator, then chase investors, angels or Santa Claus is the model, then I say no wonder there are so many failures within just years of start-up. I just do not believe the emphasis on this model sends a beginning hopeful forward with the right frame of mind needed to live long term.

Incubators have few, if any, paid professionals on staff but turn out programs, conferences, and the like, tout get togethers, all of which seems to be their real mission. There is little mention of formed businesses themselves. Those doing all this are usually young, teach various classroom elements on starting, running, and growing a business, but have never done so themselves nor have the bona fides. Go figure. Incubators should demand a buy-in from participants instead of floating them with government subsidies. Incubators themselves should have a for-profit model with paid professional staff. This would parallel real life which is why its participants are there. There should be longevity programs of two and three years venturing into the zones where businesses start collapsing. Non-profits do good things but demonstrating for-profit capitalism is probably not one of them.

Incubators are somewhat different from accelerators. Incubators primarily collect rent and provide some contacts and instruction. They have little paid staff and pull together community volunteers to help mentor. Accelerators go further with light funding of $15,000 to $50,000. But even with that one has to ask "accelerate what?" If the goal is to accelerate something that creates new jobs and creates new things, here is an idea. Provide *existing* businesses with this same accelerated ju ju which would be a much more stable platform in which to invest. The desired growth results should be better and the failure rate smaller.

Start-ups would benefit more from taking extra time than hurrying up. Entrepreneurship is more of a distance run than a sprint and I don't understand the hurry-up. Perhaps it is because each party is running through thin funding at an equally fast rate. Developing entrepreneurs should take things at their pace and not be gee hawed into time tables set by people with programs. The goal of incubators and accelerators seems to be: Whaaa Laaaa...Instant Entrepreneur! This is not very realistic.

To me, this is putting the cart before the horse. If you have no money you cannot start a business nor have any business starting one. Wait until you do. The quick launchers would do well to demonstrate long term successes that show fast track, no-money-on-hand, beg-for-it approaches produce lasting results. Author Jason Fried cautions on this when he says "Start a business not a start up." I could not agree more. What is needed more than business incubators are business sustainers. They would make a much more needed contribution to entrepreneurship than incubators or even putting more new businesses into orbit. I would think programs directed to sustainability would have a much better following and contribute in a more meaningful way to entrepreneurship in general.

Incubators like holding "boot camps," a curious name for any course in entrepreneurship. I have been through a real one and the idea is to crush any spirit of the individual and subordinate to command. Any display of creativity gets 1000 push-ups. One size fits all is the boot camp way. Entrepreneurship is about 180 degrees in the opposite direction of that philosophy.

If I was incubating or accelerating I would do it differently and self-incubate. I would look around the industry I am trying to enter and partner with an established business already somewhat in your same interest. The assumption is you would bring something to this business it could sell to its existing customers thus enhancing their offering as well as bringing a market for your new thing. Or, you might bring some new knowledge and enthusiasm to the host that it could use to start a new offering with you on the lead.

It doing this you would likely not be paying rent and may get a small salary as you incubate/accelerate or apprentice. You would learn about business first hand, much more real than from an incubator, and from a real owner. This partnership may be enough to get you going and in effect, replace your need for working capital. Who knows what possibilities might develop?

Boot Strappers Live Longest

Starting up means rustling seed money which is usually a sticking point. Neophytes discover banks don't loan on passion for ideas. Investors want a piece of the business. Family lenders come with pressure and endanger the family. Well boo hoo. As a business owner facing financial challenges is commonplace with cash shortages, credit denials, drops in business, slow inventory turns, problems collecting AR, and all the rest. If you can't produce your own money at the outset what makes anyone think you can handle the many future cash problems in small business? Show us the money.

When I started in 1981 I put in $15,000 ($50,000 today) and never put in any more. I built a 3 million dollar business that could get a bank loan when needed and paid me $250,000 a year. In 1999 I put in $65,000, along with a partner doing the same, to start the Kawasaki dealership. We never put in any more building up to 2.5 million in revenue. In both cases, with the clock ticking, the main motivation was to *sell like hell* and we did.

Bootstrapping a start-up with the combination of owner funds and salepreneur skills produces the highest success rate and the purity of ownership. Noted entrepreneur Mark Cuban puts it well:

"Argh. Write it down. Sweat equity is the best equity. When you take money from someone else, you're beholden to them. When you borrow money from a bank, if you don't meet their payments, they own you. People think that it's all about connections and money when it comes to starting or running a company when in reality, most companies fail not for lack of cash but for lack of brains."

Well said Mark.

Most long lasting entrepreneurs start self-funded by bootstrapping and are better for it. They created their own start up funds, their own cash flow, and did not look to anyone else. They chopped wood and built sweat equity. You recall the story of the fish vs. the fisherman: "Give a man a fish and he eats for a day. Teach him to fish and he feeds himself for a lifetime." Entrepreneurs who build lasting businesses to nourish themselves come knowing how to fish. Some may disagree but securing an investor, angel, or silent partner forfeits owning your own business, the original goal, and someone is just giving you fish. These outsiders will control. Should you take significant investors insist they come with the business acumen to teach fishing. Investors make the most sense for larger businesses.

Small upstarts are usually so small it should be within their owner's power, passion, and finances to start up if he actually possesses business ability. Save your own money or get a bank loan and then you own it outright. It shows you possess business ability, eliminates outsiders who ruin your fun and says you own your business. Owning your own business was the original idea, right?

Let's try and be more specific. If you are a one man startup you should have $50,000 of cash and credit line. Within six months you should be attaining break-even from salepreneur efforts including some pay. Otherwise, what you are doing may not be that viable. Sometimes you hear an upstart should have enough money to go one year without pay but that is too long.

Those seeking funding, meaning those wanting to sell off the financial risk at the outset, do not meet the definition of an entrepreneur which, again, means putting your own funds at risk. I don't understand why funding seekers do not just hitch up their pants and go sell their products they believe a market is just waiting to snap up. That raises funds, is in your control and puts you in a much more honorable state than being a Begapreneur. It says you can sell and bring in money. I don't see how anyone stays in business without being able to do these two things. Bootstrappers are the heroes because they get right to work hunting business, customers and sales while others spend too much valuable time hunting funding, investors or angels.

Try not to have partners to raise money, either. Some partnerships work but most, after a time, blow up the business. Partnerships begin from necessity, not desirability, and are too often smoldering volcanoes which erupt. Egos start infighting, strategy gets debated, work is no longer fun and the business begins deteriorating. Buy out partners whenever the opportunity is there to eliminate this business killer. Your real partners should be your customers and your first customer is your first investor.

Non-Equity Financing Sources

Instead of bootstrapping, a new non-loan, non-equity (that's right, you don't pay it back and they get no ownership so how cool is that?) financing method called crowd funding is absolutely the best way to get start up funds. Numerous investors chip in amounts like $20 $50 that hopefully add up to the start up cash you need. The money is not paid back and the investor does not get any ownership. The payback is expected in free product, limited editions, the fun of it, and future discounts. A leader is Kickstarter who began in 2009 and funds hundreds of projects claiming a 44% success. They keep 5% and fund through Amazon which keeps 5%. You must apply and be accepted. You submit your project via a video and state your goal of needed funds. If the amount is funded

100% by the crowd, the funder then charges all the supporters' credit cards, keeps their 5% and sends you the rest. If the goal is not met you do not get anything.

The SBA is an excellent source for business loans that a bank considers too risky such as those for starting a business. The SBA does not lend money but guarantees loans, up to 75%, made by a local participating SBA bank. This includes loans for land and building and pricey equipment. Regular credit worthiness applies and, if you have it, the SBA backs you by guaranteeing 75% of your loan making it attractive for the bank to loan. Why would they do this? Well, your tax dollars at work is one answer. Another is to help the economy grow. Still another is that a business is a tax collecting machine making it a good government customer. It generates sales tax for them, FICA, SUTA,FUTA, property tax, income tax, gross receipts tax, franchise and excise tax, Medicare and Medicaid payments, and that is just on the business. They get similar tax revenue from employees' checks. The U.S. Treasury loves you.

Buy Instead of Start?

A less risky, less stressful way than starting cold is buying a business. Buying a business nets a known entity that has done the building leasing, furniture buying, outfitting, hiring and development of a customer base. You dig right in doing what you know best, hopefully increasing customers and revenues, applying your expertise, and not eating mental and working capital on the rest.

Another version is buying in partially in a minority role with plans to own 100%—the route I took. I did that, not to minimize risk but to get into a business I knew. I negotiated in as the third minority partner which turned majority two years later. Minority stakes do not have much say and clout only comes at 51% ownership. A couple major points on my story: 1) I went to them, they were never going to find me and 2) I went after an environment tailored to my experience.

Buying a business usually requires some owner financing. The seller can repossess the business should you default and you forfeit what you paid (see last chapter on pricing a business). While buying a business reduces start up stress it adds the stress of managing the large debt to buy it.

If you still insist on starting a business while not an expert, while unschooled, then buy a franchise. Franchisors are already experts and don't mind getting others to participate for a fee and royalties. It is not a bad way to go. In effect, franchises have already done the selling for you by building their brand with expensive advertising. Customers know the name and trust it increasing the chances they come. Franchises have lower failure rates than start ups. If they have a good name it is easier to obtain a working capital loan or perhaps the franchisor even extends one. Franchises are easier to resell. If you are successful at one location they scale easier to multiple locations. Select one in your area of expertise and one that fits your traits.

Whatever your option it won't happen overnight. Buying a business is not a simple process and takes three months, if not six, and involves lawyers. Take the time to get the right one. If you find yourself rushing into it make yourself stop. Time is your friend here so take it.

Entrepreneurship By Santa Claus

It is a caution zone when organizations call for ideas and have programs to pitch them within five minutes to investors. I guess others can argue this has business merit but not soundly. It's throwing something on the wall and hope it sticks. Someone with real business talent and expertise should not have to be jumping up and down in front of investors to get their business going. This is entrepreneurship-by-Santa-Claus stuff and there is an industry built around it.

Others, looking for similar gifted entrepreneurship, like to ask "why is not more done to help minority businesses or woman-owned businesses be successful? (how about all left handed owners?). " It is a silly question and non-starter asked mostly by those benefiting politically.

Might as well ask why is not more done to help people become Navy SEALS? Airline pilots? PhD's? NFL quarterbacks? They are minorities too. Because you can't. Small business advocacy groups whine about things they want…. "banks need to loan more … the government should do more … we should get more contracts because we are small" and blah, blah, blah, but the solution to these problems and to elevating your 'preneur path is doing more business. You have to do that and not Santa. Nobody can do it for you. Change "where's mine?" thinking to "here's mine!" as you show the fruits of your efforts.

The emphasis for bare cupboard wana-bees is sometimes to flip the embryo for cash once traction is gained. The strategy is not long term but more Business Blackjack. Between no money wanatpreneurs begging funding, quick-pitchers, give-us-preference female groups, give-us-preference minority owner groups, and the flippers, it looks like entrepreneurship-by-Santa-Claus is rising instead of how it came to be admired which was by earning it. If you think you get business because of your age, sex or race you are not entrepreneurial material or awake in the 21st century. If Santa does visit you, in any case, it won't be on a sustained basis.

The marketplace could care less if you are male, female, black, white, Asian, Hispanic, Alaskan, young, old, tall, short, or a cry baby. Most customers do not check those categories before purchasing. Businesses not in a minority lose plenty of business and it is doubtful what they do get is because they are in a majority. They just know how to do it and go do it. Business success functions within this meritocracy and success is rarely gifted. But, to be in any way negative against the budding is akin to being against new born babies and the Fourth of July. The best thing is to keep it real. It doesn't get any easier ahead.

So there is ballyhoo about starting businesses but that is not the real story of entrepreneurship. Staying in business is! There should be more headlines about businesses lasting five years and ten than those starting. Again, staying in business is the hard part. Anyone can start one which does not mean much more than someone saying they are starting to learn the piano. OK, come back when you have something you can play. Wantapreneurs to bet on are those assuming responsibility for success using their efforts, their money, are not willing to give that up to someone else, and have the right stuff. The easier people try to make it on you to succeed the worse you end up. It ends as it begins, remember?

The Real Ones

Those I see succeed dress well, exercise, are financially disciplined, use their money, call on a lot of customers, can sell, depend upon themselves, do their heavy lifting and chop wood. Some examples: Noah Figueroa worked at a rail road repair company when he noticed farmers asking to buy old flatbed railroad cars to make inexpensive bridges on their farmland. Noah, a welder, began buying them and welding them to farmers' needs and now does this in 38 states. There is Henry Williams, a former car sales manager who noticed you could buy expensive equipment cheaply from government surplus at Govliquidation.com. He always wanted a coffee farm and bought pumps, generators, and a tractor from this site, installed it all, and now sells thousands of bags of coffee. These are both hands on guys who did anything, used their own money, did the heavy lifting, made the sales calls, and later hired help. That's how it works best and how it starts for most business owners.

While incubators and accelerators may work with 15 companies check your local business papers under "New Business Licenses" or "New Incorporations" to see the hundreds, even thousands, of new yearly start-ups that begin unheralded and without headlines. They are fueled by sweat equity just like these two guys. These fledgling owners don't have their hands out which stay in their own pockets. Working from salepreneur mode, they create their own funds and headlines. Last year in Memphis there were over 750 start-ups like these.

Because of the uniqueness required, and nuclear work ethic, no one should be encouraged into entrepreneurship anymore than the priesthood. Deciding for entrepreneurship has to be your well considered decision. If you have the right characteristics, bring the expertise and choose your market very carefully, you can find substantial job satisfaction and financial reward. But no amount of rah rah is going to get you there.

If there was an acid test to know if you could make it in ownership I have one. Find sales work with a product or service you like. See if you can make a living selling it on straight commission. Those are similar conditions faced as a new business owner. If you think you are an entrepreneur, or think it might be for you, making successful sales calls is a good test. Ask yourself 1) does anyone need this? 2) do I know where to find them? And 3) can I successfully show why they need it? If yes to all those, go out and do it tomorrow.

If you can't or won't, then you are not ready. Only you know, and can know, if you should pursue entrepreneurship. See if anyone egging you on has a vested interest in doing so. It is too complex and life changing to rest in anyone's hands but yours. This must be your own well considered decision. Take your time. Serve an apprenticeship that provides an avenue to take over the business.

From Inc. Magazine

A recent editorial by the editor of *Inc.* magazine, a national publication for entrepreneurs, provides a summary of some of what it takes to be a business owner:

> *"Long before I joined Inc. I was an actor. That profession was probably the worst preparation for covering entrepreneurship except for this: Many more want to be actors than will ever succeed at it. Indeed, the market of unemployed actors is large enough to support a bustling industry of teachers, coaches, and agents. At their best, these businesses teach aspiring actors skills and filter lucky ones into paying endeavors. At their worst they merely provide a fantasy camp.*
>
> *The supply-demand mismatch is at least as severe for entrepreneurs as for actors. That is especially true today, in the era of what Thom Ruhe, VP of entrepreneurship at Kauffman, calls "positive brand confusion" over business ownership as an easy, glamorous path to riches. As in showbiz, entrepreneurship's aspirational fringe has its own enabling ecosystem: university*

courses, accelerators, affinity groups, and a bottomless supply of pitch contests.

I don't think for a moment they are scams. But I do wonder whether some opt for the entrepreneurship "experience" over the lonely, exhausting and terrifying real thing. It is nearly impossible to succeed in entrepreneurship if you do not go all in. "Unless there are real consequences for failure, until you have personally guaranteed a line of credit and tried to sell your product to an actual human," says Ruhe, you won't have the motivation needed to build a business. Companies get built in the spaces between you, your customers, your investors, your vendors and your team, where things get gritty and complicated and rarely go according to plan. They do not get built, unfortunately, on a pitch-contest stage."

Most businesses are not built, nor sustained, without serious sweating including the start-up financing. I usually say "uh oh" when a budding entrepreneur seeks outside funding, venture capital, or angels to launch his idea instead of his own money or bank loan. It really does not meet the entrepreneurship definition which says you put your own money at risk. If a wantapreneur brings little cash to the table he should leave the table. The wantapreneur will take things more seriously with skin in the game and try harder. I learned from renting homes, for example, that if a renter could not raise a deposit I would have cash flow problems the rest of the way but not so with those who could.

The Real Work

We have established the need to know what you are doing and to be an expert at something. The main import of that is it gives you a base to progress to the real work of an entrepreneur which is to uncover new opportunities in your industry or even outside of it. The completion of your apprenticeship and establishment of a business structure speaks of your abilities but that is far from the end of the show. Times change, businesses change, marketplaces change, your enthusiasm levels change and all this has to be met with new adaptive stuff from you. This is the zone where full entrepreneurship plays out as you adjust and innovate amazing new twists to your business.

The ultimate goal of entrepreneurship is to work mostly in this new zone and not so much practicing the expertise that got you there. This is the classic junction where you work "on" the business and not "in" it. In place of practicing your expertise, now delegated, you practice entrepreneurship. This theme will be developed throughout the book. Here is my resume on this: after establishing a base of business, I bought four small copier companies, opened two copy shops, bought a copy shop, wrote two business books, opened an office in Nashville and sold it later, opened Kawasaki of Memphis and sold it eight years later, opened a medical division and a filtered drinking water business. That is where my 'preneur path led while working on the business and actualizing my inner entrepreneur.

Heavy Lifting Required

In this gig you are not getting out of the heavy commitment, uncertain outlook, wood-chopping duties, nor the need for wearing big boy pants most of the time. There is no path to business success labeled Entrepreneurship Lite. You are the one who has to know how to do the hard stuff like open the mouths of alligators or push a string. Solving everyday problems like collections or inventory management are to be left to mere mortals while you learn to, say, fly a jet in a gymnasium.

Think about shows whose principles deal with conquering adversity like Ice Road Truckers, Dirty Jobs, Dangerous Drives, A Minute To Win It, Undercover Boss, Alaskan State Troopers, Nat Geo Wild and Bear Grylles survival stories to get the proper frame. MacGyver is your role model. I love this Facebook posting by a Paul Carney, from which I took his phrase that speaks to the entrepreneurial work ethic: "You would have fewer problems with teens if they had to chop wood to keep their smart phones going." Are you willing to chop a lot of wood to earn your entrepreneurial keep? Chop! Chop!

It is not enough to be expert in your craft. That earns you a job but not command of a business which requires serious weightlifting ability. What do you do if an important contract cancels? Your product is commoditized? What do you do if running out of money? If an employee embezzles? What do you do if audited? What if you are being sued? What if you and your partner make each other miserable? What if you have a nut case competitor? What do you do if enthusiasm is waning?

You have to be the captain who can deal with incoming, operate the sonar, the radar, fire the guns, understand the power plant, all the operational things, *and* successfully navigate combatants trying to sink him! Captains earn their stripes by missing the icebergs, surviving the storm, preventing a mutiny, not getting lost, and conquering all come what may. Either that or walk the plank mate. (Yes, I was in the Navy.)

Lesson From Alaska

I saw a movie that forms a metaphor for adversity in business and using creativity to solve snags. In Barrow, Alaska winter came early and was quickly freezing ice that trapped three whales. Whales cannot stay underwater indefinitely like a fish and must be able surface regularly to breath. Their only air opening in the ice was 100 square yards and the ocean's freedom lie five miles away. An environmental group began using chain saws to keep the hole open. News covered it and an industrialist volunteered his ice cutting barge some fifty miles away. But the ice was closing. Numerous locals were recruited and began turning out to cut sequential holes. It would require about fifty holes to lead the whales to the ocean. It was next reported that the ice-cutting barge was hopelessly far away. The next day brought a blizzard and little work could be done. One whale died.

The mayor appealed for any icebreaking ship that could help. A Russian ship was nearby but required clearance from the White House. Meanwhile, locals kept digging holes and the two whales followed each hole closer and closer to the sea. Their ice cutting tools eventually dulled and new ones had to be flown in. In a few days President Ronald Reagan expedited the arrival of the Russian cutter which rammed the ice but got stuck. The locals began cutting away the ice the ship was hung on and freed it. The ship took another run at it and that did it. The two whales made it. Yay!

Yes, that is about right. In this true story the whales represent your business and its own quest for survival. The inventive locals represent you and your employees. You need to be as creative as those locals and just as determined, especially when you have a whale-sized problem.

In the meantime, sharpen your business tools. Understand the importance of working capital and how much to have, how to maintain positive cash flow, to price right, to obtain a bank loan, to make a profit, to lead, to make sales, to overcome, to understand ratios, to interpret financial statements. This takes a few years. It's what makes a business person. If you are not learning these then you're not serious and maybe ownership is not for you.

If you relish creating ideas, floating them, discussing them, but the business of business does not motivate you, then get a job where your skills are fungible like an inventor, teacher, speaker, writer, or maybe syndicate your expertise. Perhaps better to pitch yourself to a business that takes on your idea and lets you concentrate on that while it handles business. You may create a new department or profit center and everyone is happy. If you want to be a business owner the business of business must interest you.

Do Something!

"There is only do or not do. There is not try"—Yoda. This is so particularly true as the acid test in business. Maybe the most important expertise of them all is *doer-ship*. Entrepreneurship is about doing. Doing it now. Doing it yourself. Doing it again. Doing it better. Doing it under duress. Doing it when you don't want to. Doing it until failure and then doing it some more. Do or die works. Entrepreneurship is a noun but should be a verb. I remember from spelling class: "Children, verbs are doing words."

Here is my doing resume, an elevator pitch to my habits of entrepreneurship: I started with my own money, made thousands of sales calls, drove thousands of miles, composed hundreds of proposals, changed hundreds of proposals, made a zillion phone calls, many not returned, got good advice and not so good, wore out shoes, wore out pants, hired people, fired people, encouraged people, helped people, had money, lost money, spent good money and bad on advertising, gained some large accounts, lost some large accounts, made sales and lost sales, had an embezzler, worked with some mean employees, some hard chargers and some lazy ones, had times when I was happy and times I hated it, times I paid bills easily and times I was late, times when I won recognition and times I wouldn't qualify, days when I left early and days when I stayed late, nights when I slept well and nights I didn't sleep, been to court and lost, been to court and won, sold a few companies, bought a few, started a few, jogged thousands of miles for stress management, and am married with kids and animals. That is my doing resume. When you accept business ownership you say "I dooooooo!"

Entrepreneurship is about execution of the action. Taking action, any action, is a good plan because it leads to more discovery and new brain neurons connecting resulting in progress or inspiration. *Motion creates emotion* which in turn, puts gas in the tank. Picture the determined NFL running back. His plan is to make the end zone but he cannot really draw up how until he gets going, then zigging from hounding pursuers, then realizing he needs some zagging quickly learned from the zigging. It's the same for you. Actions reap. No excuses. In the south we have procrastination terminology for this like "I am fixn' to … I'm planning on it … I'm gettn' around to it … or talk is cheap." Then there is our riddle of three toads on a log. Two decide to jump off. How many does that leave? Still three because deciding and doing are different things.

Who To Listen To

This brings up the cautionary tale of who to listen to for business advice. My answer: those not in the advice business. The best source is probably your customers. Poll a cross section. Ask them what it will take to keep their business and get more of it. Ask them how you look in comparison to competitors. In my opinion there is a lack of credibility in the business advice business and it has elements of puffery and hollowness. Many in it have never run or grown a real business. I admire a business Ph.D at our university who makes no bones about never owning a business so in her entrepreneurship curriculum she turns some classes over to entrepreneurs. "I want students to hear from real ones," she says.

I saw a movie on the Military Channel that helps here. A sergeant was to give a class on hypothermia but instead told students to report to a warehouse where he had a tub of ice water. He told them to strip and get in. For 15 minutes they shivered, suffered, turned blue and began to lose cognitive ability. A captain happened by: "Sergeant, what the hell are you doing to these men." The sergeant replied "I was to teach them about hypothermia today, sir, so instead of speaking to them in a classroom they are getting the experience of my experience." The captain approved and after 15 minutes in the tub the sergeant barked "class dismissed."

If you want valuable advice look to those who have swam in ice water! Now if I knew someone with a bad experience in a sauna I would have both ends covered. Wantapreneurs are vulnerable and suggestible and the best thing we can do for them is keep them in touch with reality and tone down the carnival barking.

I have seen those talking, coaching, advising, and consulting with business owners, holding themselves out as gurus, but never successfully operated a business yet lecture as if they took Google public. They are largely self-appointed and self-anointed. When you pull back their curtain you may see the Wizard of Oz, and only the Wizard, spinning his record. Some Wizards use other's material, making them mostly recyclers and cheerleaders. Again, you can't give what you don't have and make sure anyone advising you has the credentials for what you seek.

There is even a franchise called The Growth Coach. The reason one would buy a franchise for this is that they never had a real business themselves. Ouch! No established owner would seek growth advice from somebody who bought a franchise about it. That is how low we have sunk in the business advice business.

I cringe seeing a supposed authority with, drum roll, wait for it, "The Three C's You Must Never Forget!" Or "The One Thing To

Always Remember!" Or "Do These Two Things and Increase Sales by a Gazillion!" It is the equivalent of saying: "To prevent a heart attack do this one thing—don't eat bacon." Business health, like heart health, is way more complicated. But some are hungry to find things to say and over reach their station.

Beware of those using lofty words like convergence, fusion, paradigms, throughput, alignments, dynamics, existential, and entrepreneurial ecosystems. I have recently seen "client attraction system" (marketing in English).

All meaningful business terms are well known and simple enough. No real business owner speaks in these terms and those that do are doing so for their notoriety more than your benefit. If I asked you what some of these words meant, if like me even as a journalist by education, I don't know what they are talking about. Which is the idea, so that you have to pay to listen to someone explain them who may presume you are borderline illiterate. I could respond to such language saying "these speakers use abstruse vocabulary and are being esoteric." Or, restate this: "the speaker uses vocabulary difficult to understand and wording understood by only a few. Which sentence communicates to you? Buyer beware and look for entrepreneurial authenticity in advisors who avoid the full opera shows and speak simply from lived experience.

Business writers are sometimes woefully unschooled in business. They may have a degree in journalism but not much experience in the workings of business. Even so, you would expect that they would research topics, find the facts, figures and quantitative data to background their subject. But, usually business writers, especially at local publications, take the word of their interviewee and quote his stuff as factual. This is not journalism and does not serve readers. A good writer should have the business knowledge to separate self serving PR from actual business fact. But often they don't. They need a story to fill tomorrow's space and checking facts and background takes time. The good news is the more national publications specializing in business give you that.

I don't like advisors who, although I do this some, speak about how large and successful companies do things. You *can* take from them concepts or principles to apply to your business. But, you simply cannot execute the way they do because they have endless money, credit, reputation, leverage and talent you don't. You have to execute with what you have and that is not the same as Federal Express or Google. You want advisors who know how to do it with small means because that is you. Keep that reality in mind, don't listen long about how big boys do things but do learn their concepts which can aid creative thinking.

To get sound data on entrepreneurship go with the Kauffman Foundation. They are quite serious about it. A decent source for individual counsel is SCORE which stands for the Service Corps of Retired Executives. You can be sure these people have had real business experience. They are all volunteers so results may vary but their services are free aside from some workshops open to the public.

Coach vs. Consultant

It is important to understand the difference between a coach and a consultant. Both can bring some needed help to you if they are not pseudo. A coach helps you do things you should be doing but aren't—a sort of Rent-A-Boss for bosses. It could be your spouse. A consultant is a specialized expert used when you do not know what or how to do something. Do some vetting before staking yourself on what somebody says. If you find a person willing to mentor, that you admire and can communicate with, offer a monthly retainer of $250-$500. This should give you valuable access when you need it and be the least expensive person you ever hire.

If going into battle would you rather listen to a combat veteran or motivational coach? A pilot who has flown or only been in a simulator? If a coach talks about hiring him to grow your business ask how he is growing his own and how many employees he hired recently. I cannot think of a more highly in-demand person than someone effective in growing businesses. Common sense would say if a grow-your-business-guru is effective he would have one of the highest growth businesses around, and certainly one bigger than one or two people, since he is about showing everyone how to make more money. But they don't because they don't. In business the scorecard is money so ask gurus to show you the money they produced.

That said, I do believe a coach could become proficient and helpful in a specified area without the business experience such as leadership training, crises management, finance, salesmanship and the like. For a consultant/coach to be a real "business" coach, to advise on growing your business, the acid test is familiarity with finance meaning he can comfortably walk through financial statements, ratios in chapter 7, and understand a business acquisition. Business is about the numbers and whoever is advising better be able to lift the hood on your business to understand where you are.

Be Skeptical

Be careful about biting on seminars that promise lofty things. Most messages boil to "Be nice to customers," "You can do it!" and "Work Hard!" Not exactly stuff you didn't know. Sloganeering never solved a business problem though it made you feel better for a day, perhaps two. I hate the rallies when celebrities come to "speak" and inspire you to greatness. It may be Terry Bradshaw combined with Laura Bush or whoever. Inspiration doesn't hurt but *none of these people do what you do*. You do not have their fame working for you, either, which makes everything they do a lot easier than it ever will be for you. Spend elsewhere.

Know that good speakers are good, first of all, because they speak well in public. That is a skill and art in itself. It does not mean those with the skill are actually putting out what the audience needs. Probably those with the best first hand information are not those trying to earn a living with regular speaking gigs. You would like to see The World's Greatest Small Businessperson' turn into The World's Greatest Speaker. That would be somebody to listen to!

Another caution are speakers building a following by declaring something is dead. "Blah, blah, blah is dead and it is because I say so!" If it is dead it is doubtful we don't already know about it. If we don't already know that it is also likely the thing is not dead. Attend seminars on public speaking, marketing methods, sales techniques, interpreting financial statements, pricing correctly or mastery of useful software. These are the muscle building things owners really need. Find meaningful business knowledge from those living it—owners with resumes. They will likely answer questions free if you respect their time.

Form a Five Group. This peer group of five owners meets monthly to discuss problems hoping peers have ideas and answers. True confession time. The group should not have competitors and at each meeting financial statements are examined for trends. This is authentic help that requires trust, but, as I say, is where the best advice lives. I repeat—it never ceases to amaze how some, holding out as coaches, consultants, instructors, gurus, and the rest, never owned, operated, or grew a business. Perhaps this is one reason failures are high because there is a lack of authenticity in the advice/education business. The facts behind many failures are that would be entrepreneurs are ill prepared and most advisers are as well.

Be skeptical about "best-selling authors". Have you noticed most are Best-Selling? A real best-selling author makes the New York Times best-selling list. To be an Amazon bestseller all that is required is a book be in the top 100 sellers, in its category, for one day. You be the judge. This does not mean the book does not have merit.

For helpful reads subscribe to the *Economist,* one of the best magazine's there is, *Inc.* magazine, *Entrepreneur* magazine, and Jim Blasingame's column *The Small Business Advocate.* Take *in Al's Emporium* in the Sunday Wall Street Journal and Neil Cavuto on Fox. Heck, search my column archives at memphisdailynews.com and put Tom Pease in the search box to view 100 columns of small business advice. Of course you will want to keep this book by your bedside. There are business lessons in *Shark Tank* and *The Apprentice*

Reprinted below is one of my columns from The Daily News that speaks tongue-in-cheek to our subject.

Determining The Best Business Book
By Tom Pease

All business owners are on search for anything that helps them. They quickly buy books that shout "The Eight Things You Must Know" or "The Seven Habits You Must Have" or "The One Thing To Get Right". There are numerous "Four Volume CD Sets You Must Listen To." There might be the "Three 'T's To Always Remember." Writers need a hook to catch attention and business people like numbers so is this the best formula to sell business books?

Steven Covey wrote the really successful The Seven Habits of Highly Successful People. But it is 358 pages! That is 51.1 pages per habit. The One Minute Manager is only 100 pages but still takes hours to read. How can we be good minute managers if it takes hours to understand? Shouldn't we be able to read it in minutes? Tom Peters released 163 Ways To Pursue Excellence. Say what? Can you get it down to 11 ways for us Tom? This is Twitter Nation and you are way past your 140 characters. There is 15 Ways To Take Control of Your Career Now. If we combine those with Tom's 163 ways we have 178 ways to do it. Napoleon Hill wrote The Law of Success in Sixteen Lessons. Would his 16 lessons be contained in Peter's 163 ways because that would keep us from buying and reading three books. Maybe somebody could write 100 Ways to Make Money and rebate 90 to get us to 10 we would read.

All books have helpful information but, of course, there are no certain number of things. Many books say the same things but have different hooks. There are only the right things for you however many. It is being able to DO them that is the hard part. All the knowledge in the world won't do you any good if you won't use it.

Book titles today are frequently one word. There is Switch, Fish, Rework and E Myth. This could be because one word is the most tweetable or is all anyone can remember. Having written a book with a long title I wondered what my next book title might be if it was one word. "Chameleon" comes to mind. It makes perfect sense since you have to be like one, able to adapt and change with your environment to stay alive in business. The chameleon goes way back in time but so does the cockroach which came over on the Ark. These two critters have merit as examples of the staying power a business needs but are ugly and creepy so will not do for our title.

I am a motor head so I thought about engine metaphors. I have it! "Diesel". A diesel is efficient, lasts longer than other engines and carries the heaviest loads. Business owners must do that. But diesel has a bad connotation of dirty and polluting so this would cost book sales and be a bad image. Sports analogies are always good. "Win!". "Do It!". "Sweat! "Want It!". "Practice!?". "Home Run!". "No. 1!". Getting close but sports also have so much tragedy and disappointment. You could just as well throw out "Loser!". "Concussion!". "Foul!". "Interception!". Those could hurt book sales although they tell the troubles business owners encounter.

I love dogs so let's look there. "Doberman!". "Retriever!". "Greyhound!". I think actual dog names work better. Maybe Goliath, Tycoon, or Sampson. All signify strength of mind and body a business owner needs so that is good. My dog's name is Moe which was one of the Three Stooges so we can't go there even if Moe was CEO of the Stooges.

My final possibility is "Flexibility", the quality Houdini had that let him escape all danger but that sounds lame. Owners face plenty of danger but that title is just boring. This title does give me license to change my mind, though, on the one-word title limit since you do have to be flexible in business. I therefore invoke the flexibility of using more than one word and arrive at my title for the best business book: "All The Above."

In conclusion, let's try to benchmark the ideal entrepreneur. It really can't be done, is more like shoveling smoke, but we attempt to for fun and grins:

- You are a gymnast, not a sumo wrestler.
- You are a diesel truck, not a Corvette.
- Have energy the size of a Mexican jumping bean field fertilized with hot sauce.
- You do not like being told what to do.
- A blank canvass looks good to you.
- If asked how you do it you have to think about it.
- You visit the shoe cobbler as often as the Apple store.
- Your brain has two settings: ON and ON.
- You believe the greatest obstacle to success is yourself.
- You can run a 5K without dying.
- You can sell.
- Your Christmas tree is still up near the end of January.
- You are not a neat-nik or organization freak.
- You sprinkle gunpowder on your corn flakes.
- You admit that at times your business looks uglier than a bullfrog with warts, tongue out and mutated fifth leg.
- When a banker asks about your positive cash flow you answer that you are positive you have no cash flow.
- You gain business insights watching your dog.
- Your product "eats and drinks" and is under contract.
- You feel you are the mole in the Whack-A-Mole game.
- You do not DWI-Decide While Intoxicated (on ego).
- Your short attention span can only be measured by a Hadron Particle Collider.
- You model after test pilots—willing to get off the ground and fall out of the air.

- You are the one that shoots Bin Laden.
- You are a quarterback not a lineman.
- You do not fold your tee shirts or iron your jeans.

Now that we have all your bona fides in order, have learned where to learn and where not to, you have the goods to deliver to customers. Let's move to the next chapter and get your product and process right!

Moe's summation: "After reading about the difficulty of becoming an entrepreneur I don't understand why everybody wants to be one so bad. I guess it is because they know they can't be a dog."

2

It Must
Be Easy

U sed to be you had a key to get into your car. Then came a keyless pad eliminating pesky keys. Pads are gone replaced by fobs so entering your car is not even that tasking. The key fob requires nothing of us except carrying it. Television sets are actually always on, even when off, so when turned on it happens instantly. Inserting credit cards to buy gas seems quick, but alas, no. It requires getting into the wallet, finding the card, using it, and putting it back. Way too much trouble so the RFID chip on your key chain is just waved at the pump. At Walgreens the clerk asked if I wanted prescriptions on Express Pay. "What's that?, I asked staring at the card swiper in front of me. "Isn't that it?" I asked. "Oh no sir. With Express Pay you do not have to swipe. We instantly put it to your card on file." Well thank goodness for saving that wear and preventing swipe elbow. Walgreens also has a prescription app that scans the barcode with your cell and calls in the refill.

Even carrying a wallet or a checkbook, is too much trouble today as smart phones store our money. Plugging in your cell wallet to recharge—so much trouble so now we just lay it on a wireless charging pad. Microsoft worked hard reducing double clicking to single clicks. Add up the hours of life that returned to us, plus the nanoseconds saved by the fob and express pay and we are turning back the clock! Are we there yet? Never. Here is the latest. Nissan banished the five second task of checking tire pressure by making their cars' horn sound when correct. There go the tire gauge manufacturers. But wait! Audi just came out with Traffic Jam Assist. Driving in bumper to bumper traffic is tedious and there is no attention left over for texting or putting on makeup. Americans can't have that so Traffic Jam Assist takes over the driving in these inconvenient situations.

Convenience! Convenience! Convenience! It has to work its way into any businesses today that wishes to stay pleasing to its customers.

When your product or process is easy begin making it easier, or else! Or else lose business is what. National Car rental, like others, used to offer various cars at various prices. Now they advertise "chose any car and go." Whoever thought we would be the bottled water generation? Just making it easy to carry water resulted in a billion dollar business that used to be largely free but, oh, a bit inconvenient? We pay more for it per gallon than gasoline but don't care because it is convenient. Easy does it! I could keep on about the tech that reduces stresses like self propelled vacuums, self parking cars or heated steering wheels.

These scintillating product benefits, well advertised, penetrate and form consumer consciences and expectations that spill over into similar expected conveniences from your business, too, no matter what it is. None of these businesses may have anything in common with yours but they set standards in customer expectations of ease and convenience etched into buyers' minds. These new raised standards are carried by customers into your business, and, indeed, wherever they go.

Ease and convenience are the top customer buying criteria. Can you meet those expectations? Ease and convenience are the most important characteristics in what you sell and how you process if you want to appeal to customers and stay in business.

"Ease and convenience are customers' top buying criteria."

Convenience and ease are what Americans value most when buying, even above price. Make it easy if you want to make it. The easiest to use product or procedure wins!

Take toothpaste tops. They were things you unscrewed but this is asking a lot of Americans so came the flip cap. Much easier. Then the arthritis cap. There is a pump dispenser if caps wear you out. All this seems silly if it did not involve millions of dollars. If selling non-flip top toothpaste you lose sales to the seemingly trivial flip cap simply because the flip is easier. "What, you still making me twist off my caps? I'm walkin." As a gift, I received a bottle of cologne. It has a *magnetized cap* so it just snatches the cap back on. Be gone tiresome twist caps. Flip caps—so yesterday. Since most bathroom caps are now non-twisters if I do come across a twist off I am positively annoyed. Don't be a twist off company in a flip cap world or suffer customer scorn and abandonment.

Entrepreneurs in Tennessee who own liquor stores are falling victim to ease and convenience selling wine. Liquor stores had been the only place to buy it and in turn, are prevented from selling beer or even a corkscrew. But it is underfoot to let grocers sell wine, for "the convenience of the consumer" say lawmakers, as they put a hit on liquor stores' profits in the name of consumer convenience.

Kentucky Fried Chicken announced a goal of making all its chicken boneless. Some is now but they state that boneless is much more convenient to eat for the customer and they want all servings to be this way for this reason. So if you are a chicken magnate you see the new convenience bar is set at "total boneless." McDonald's was in the news announcing its business had slowed some and blamed it on taking longer to serve its customers both inside and at the drive in window. Meanwhile Sonic Drive-Ins, which dispenses with any decorum whatsoever to impress you concentrating solely on your convenience and ease by bringing burgers right to your window, was increasing sales.

They Like It A Lot

We like easy opening cans, E-Z credit, easy application, easy entry and exit, easy application, and easy directions which we may read from our Lazy Boy recliner. I like J.B. Weld, a cold weld that came in two tubes you mixed to produce the magic. They figured customers may be tiring mixing two tubes so they sell it already mixed in one semi-firm tube you just knead to activate. Stamps requiring licking are fading with peel and stick replacements adding priceless nanoseconds to our lives. My new car has rain sensing wipers that start automatically when hit by water so I am saved that wear of turning them on myself. Easy sells and sells. Ease also provides a rationale to charge more and gets buyers to look past price tags.

A really creative example of easy comes from China. In their department stores space between escalators is full of bins of simple, high margin merchandise you pluck as you ride. Hey, no sense wasting shopping time riding escalators. This is the principle at checkouts that stash a bazillion items per inch to buy easily at high margins rather than stand and stare at another's groceries. No sense wasting valuable shopping time waiting to check out. Sears uses the smart phone as a cash register as does Apple. When you buy you scan it from your phone to their reader, which certifies funds, and bypass the cashier. Could this be easier?

If you sell anything surely you use Square, a small attachment for a smart phone or tablet that lets you swipe credit cards directly into your account. Will all this bring new meaning for 'pay phone'? Will anyone still be able to pay cash? Or plastic? Will the government still be able to print money? Can we still cash a check? I digress. Can you compete with this, or, more to the point, duplicate it? Can customers walk into your business and do this? When it is this easy, buyers scan three things instead of two, since it is fun and so easy. It could have consequences for you in increased profits.

When in sales school in the 70's the first thing taught about IBM products was their 'ease of operation' so back then companies had ease on their radar. It is something that appeals to human nature. It is American's most important buying criteria. Are you catering to it every way you know how? My wife gets the magazine *Real Simple*. Doubtful one would have many subscribers if called *Hard as Hell*. If you want to raise revenues and have copious customers then sell Easy Street. Does this mean Americans are lazy? Not really. The high road is Americans are, to the contrary, 'so busy' they need to counter with 'so easy'

Once Easy Make It Easier

The lesson is to review business operations—product offerings too—and make their easy factor ever more appealing. Be fast. Be easy. Be convenient. Or be gone. There are things in this category any small business can implement. Eliminate auto attendant and please God, the " listen carefully as our menu options have changed". No more voice mail abuse of customers. Answer first ring? No pushbutton menus. Paperwork one page? Live person available? Web site interactive, answers questions and takes business 24/7? All company calls forwarded to cell phones? All calls returned same day? Everyone answers every call? Names and contact numbers of staff on website? Location easy to find? Billing is accurate? Instruction quickly available? Repair people respond same day? Nobody hiding from anybody? Any directions, whether about location or assembling something, need to be clear as glass. You may be selling gasoline for a dollar a gallon but if it is too hard to locate it people will not bother.

Easy is another way of saying less time. Time saving is about productivity and productivity is profitability. The time is money thing. Things are made easier for businesses so they can be more efficient and profitable which is why the next version of Windows, Apple, SAP, or Oracle, is gobbled up (built in demand) because the anticipation is things will go quicker making us and our customers happier. Well, yea, once that bad boy is implemented.

Remember the march ever upward of micro processors? There was 286, then 386, 486, then breathlessly on to Pentium and Core Two Duo and ever awaiting whatever is next. Make it quick! Kroger has a goal of a 30 second check out wait. It had averaged four minutes which does not seem long but is an eternity today. Met Life Insurance is running a campaign advertising "Buy term life insurance with one call." Businesses making customers wait, such as doctor's offices, cable companies or airlines, flirt with self destruction.

OMG Apple 4S is out but 5 will be here within the year they say. (Heard iPhone 13 will be out in 2020). You torture yourself questioning to wait or not bearing the nearly unbearable thought of missing out on the latest easiest thing, and importantly, being able to get it instantly. "I have it so much harder than someone with a 5," you moan. You get it and the process begins anew. Well, we got the 4S and then 5 which is about getting Siri to do everything, certainly so we would not have to, making our life easier, and easier to use the iPhone ("I" stands for instant?), which was already easy, but with Siri we do not push anything, just talk, making it even easier!

Apple's success should erase all doubt about the economic power of easy. Its products do not really do too many actually new things. What they do better than anyone is take previous product categories and make them easier to use beyond anyone's imagination. Apple teaches another marketing lesson, a cousin of make it easier, and that is make it smaller. Smaller is associated with easier. Ease, and especially ease from innovative electronics, is also a form of entertainment, a bit of mind candy for us, that brings instant gratification and increased satisfaction with the thing. It is time for a degree in easy, maybe the PH.E, the E for easy of course. Oh wait, there already is, kind of, called ergonomics.

The reason things have to be easier/quicker is ever easier things create expectations of even easier things to come. This, in turn, has lowered people's willingness-to-wait time to nearly nothing. That is where we are. If you do not meet easy/fast expectations customers walk.

Line too long? A line at all? Holding on the phone? Too many pages of paperwork? Too slow getting an answer? Too slow fixing it? Too slow calling back? Too slow fixing the billing? The customer is out of there!

In this process of anticipation of easier things manufacturers provide another lesson: products with sequential numbers get anticipation built in, and the next one and the next, using higher numbers. Built in dissatisfaction? Or satisfaction with an expiration date? Is it 'never satisfied'? Whatever it is, it makes for built in demand and a business model that drives itself. As a small business owner, think about offering sequentially numbered products or levels of service either to build anticipation or to charge more for higher levels of something. Gatorade has done this. Gatorade used to be Gatorade but now is the "G Series" with formulas 01, 02, and 03.

Reinvent For More Ease

When I was a whipper Dad gave me easy lessons. I remember one when trying to get a weird looking screw, with no slot but a sort of notch, unscrewed on my bike. Mom's kitchen knife looked like it had a tip that would match this screw so I took it which is where Dad found me. "Son, don't reinvent the wheel. That is called a Phillips head screw and here is a Phillips screwdriver." Oh. Thanks Dad. Those days if something was really easy we said "easy as pie!" I hope I am not the only one that remembers that. Dad's wheel lessons meant not trying to make an easy thing hard when the hard part had already been made easy. Maybe you just didn't know it.

From all we have discussed it seems hardness is never conquered because there is money in continually making things even easier— reinventing easy. That is a business model for today.

Apple did not invent portable music. Sony Walkman did. It did not even invent the command icons it made so famous. Xerox did. Steve Jobs did not invent the personal computer. Steve Wozniak did that. What they all did was *reinvent* something by bringing it the ultimate level of easy. At least for a while until *that* gets reinvented. Sorry Dad. Just about all reinvention means taking something even well established, reinventing it, and making it easier. Reinventing something to be easier, whether a product or a service, is a powerhouse business strategy.

You can do likewise and reap results locally benefiting like the big boys. Some examples. The technology is available to repair computers over the Internet. Local computer companies, who have bought the equipment, can, via the Internet and with your assistance, go into your computer and repair problems or kill viruses. If this is you, advertise "Right Now Repair" for an edge. Here is another. It is generally perceived customer service is bad and impersonal yet a busy Memphis doctor has a waiting room attendant. As you *sit* she takes check in information, insurance, and collects co-pay and calms you. Patients never leave their chair until called by the doctor. I would advise the attendant to do the weigh in, temperature taking and blood pressure too! This personalized technique makes things easier for the patient and brings smiles.

A smiling customer is a buying customer. So the doctor's happy helper sits down next to the smiling Mr. Jones and says: "We should go ahead and schedule that colonoscopy Mr. Jones." And he might. Cha Ching. No way I would but in this relaxed state I might O.K. a treadmill test. Make it easy and make it happy, Scary Doctor, and your waiting room becomes your sales office.

Could a hospital emergency room copy this? One in Memphis has. Or the doctor copied them but one emergency room advertises no waiting. The doctor increased co-pays to cover the attendant. What a smart man, I say. He tapped into the power of easy. Surely this increases revenues for the doctor and hospital. And it is way past time for this in the medical area. It may already be too late in fact. Patients are tired of endless waiting and grumpy nurses so you have an industry primed for decline as it gets defined by inconvenience, lack of efficiency, frustration and time consumption. Anything but easy. Consequently, general practice doctors, internal medicine doctors are seeing practices dry up and selling to hospitals becoming their employee. The business is going to no-appointment nurse practitioners in Walgreens, Kroger, Target, Wal Mart and who knows where else, where you are quickly seen between aisle ten and the produce department. They make it easy!

That said, there are old school things, still effective, hard to improve, or make easier. One is the keystroke, the main input on computers or phones that harks to the telegraph. We still type even though on really trick machines. What about the wastebasket? Scotch tape? The pencil? The ballpoint pen (1888) is the same as ever, ink applied by a ball. Plain paper is still beloved even as we try to get rid of it. Paper was invented in 220 and is still a very efficient means of mass communication. Some 80% of company data is stored in the lowly manila file folder and put into a file cabinet invented in 1948. Old school and new meet humorously on a computer screen framed in Post-It notes. Legal pads, mostly only 12 inches long, are still heavily used. For all the talk of wireless the wire is still king of transmission, again, since the telegraph. Looked under your desk at that electronic spaghetti? Most telephone poles are still in use! OK, so Dad wins here.

Nation of Conveniacs

There are many department stores but Nordstrom is recognized as another zip code in customer service. They take back anything without fuss and rumored to once taken back a set of tires even though they don't sell them. Nordstrom gives the floor rep authority over any sale or decision to do something to please a customer. This maniacal service, in the name of ultimate convenience for the customer, takes the focus off price and nets great margins. So that is their difference.

Going to Blockbuster was easy but Netflix re-invented and only required travel to the mailbox so Blockbuster closed. There were many auto parts stores when Auto Zone arrived. They saw how inconvenient existing stores were with countermen ensconced behind the counter staring at computers as you talked. Auto Zone came out from behind the counter and is willing to install the new wiper or battery in the parking lot. They offer free testing of alternators or batteries to make sure you need one. They greet you in the aisles and ask if you needed help. No rocket science here, just making it easy to do business. Auto Zone is now the big dog and its stock is $393.

These examples demonstrate the power of providing convenience to customers and how that translates into big revenue. Let's face it, we are a nation of "conveniacs" and can never be served fast enough. You can add speed and convenience to the customer experience locally and benefit like the big boys. Businesses doing that best take business from ones that aren't.

We are a nation of multi-taskers, two families, two jobs, live in relatives, unemployed relatives, beloved dogs, payments to make, games to attend, homework to help with, on and on, more stressed than ever, so we gravitate to easy. We are older, living longer, so ease leaps up the charts as a buying criterion the older you get. I am an example of that. I have a small post office in my city but bypass it to send mail because one more out of the way has a drive up drop so I don't have to get out of the car. So the ease element of a drive up changes behavior, especially for us semi-lazy types.

Easy to do stuff makes using the thing more enjoyable too. Nobody likes a hassle so if it is the opposite we love it. If a product, process or place of business is easy to deal with this increases customer satisfaction and repeat business. If there is anything, *anything*, hard it means lost business. Staples understands and advertises their Easy Button. Whatever product or service you sell must contain elements of making life easier.

Combine Things For New Ease

Some of the biggest entrepreneurial successes come from combining existing elements that never have been. Nobody in their wildest imagination, no far seeing executive, ever said: "One day, your telephone will combine with your camera." Yet today, cell phones have cameras about as good as they get and put a crater in camera sales and the film business. Why? Because camera phones are so darn easy, easy to carry, easy to use. We have *always had* cameras it's just nobody phoned them in for ultimate convenience. There is the power of easy again and giving new meaning to "take it easy."

We are used to UPS to our door but combine home delivery with pizza? We can drive in and out for oil changes but now eyeglasses or dentures in an hour? Telephones and Internet? Medical care and grocery shopping? Mail boxes and movies? Parking lots and car washes? Teleconferencing and college degrees? Bookstores and café's? Women's hair salons and wine? Here is a completely new combination to sell cars. Chrysler has come up with selling its Dart through bridal registry. One person pays for the motor, another the interior, another the wheels, until the car is paid for.

A Memphis gas station added an attendant to pump gas for those wanting this convenience. He is paid like a waiter, small salary and tips, and draws a niche group of senior and handicap customers so you have a gas station combined with a waiter. New industries are created combining elements not before combined that make things ever easier. Ask yourself what stand-alone elements you could combine, that never have been, to create something new. As you walk the aisles of any store picture combining items on the left side with some on the right and see if you come up with something interesting.

Sometimes techno-combines stupefy how they change an industry by making things easier. Remember going to the bank? Used to take your checks and wait in line or drive through to deposit them. Not anymore. A desk top scanner combines with checks which deposits them saving time and gas. Banks are asking why they built branches to come to when no one is. Boo hoo. Be looking for ways, like banks, to implement technology to make doing business with you hard to resist. Maybe you should be selling it too!

In my industry customers call in a monthly meter, call for service and supplies. Now they don't. The copiers combine with the Internet and have software that automatically emails my dealership when the machine is low on toner or needs service. It also emails the meter reading with no human intervention. Easy! This adds for large companies with many machines. They like us for making things easier and are impressed by our technology.

The point is you don't have to invent some totally new moon shot product to be a great entrepreneur. Like companies mentioned simply (simply?) take a piece of the *process* and reinvent it to be easier. If you cannot reinvent it yourself find someone that already has and sell that. There are enough successful examples of this to prove it is a powerful business model and one you should be using. What is your "Easy As Pie" plan?

In 1980's John Naisbitt coined the phrase "High tech, high touch" in *Megatrends* which is still true, but maybe update it to "High stress, high convenience".

Nothing Easier Than Free

There is nothing easier than getting something free. Or at least the perception it is free, works. It is true to a point, but these offers always come with treble fish hooks to make you pay *something*. This is the age of 'free' to lure you. I think it works and owners are advised to look hard at it. The idea is that the cost of giving free product would replace paying for advertising or media. Either way you pay. It is the advertising industry that takes the hit.

We are not talking free parking, free trial, free coffee, free Wi-Fi, free credit report or free advice either although those do attract. Nor are we mentioning no payments for a year or 60 months free interest. We are talking free product. Take books, which take months to write. Authors are encouraged to give talks and spill all their goods from the book, as well as give everyone there a free copy, in order to sell more books. I have written over 100 articles for a local paper, each takes about three hours, and must be free to the newspaper whose thinking is the author benefits from the publicity.

I responded to a free website ad by Go Daddy. I have a product I wanted to experiment with and web design gets pricey. A one page site was free but, not having looked into web costs recently, you still pay to host, for a shopping cart, and email. Pay! Blah, blah, blah and my AMEX was $545 for my free website. So free can be effective and there are plenty of examples like Go Daddy. But relying on free is expensive and means you are getting lazy in your sales efforts. Profit margins slip because of that as well as pricing discipline. Customers are not stupid either and know there is a cost in there somewhere. If you use free then whatever this free stuff is needs to set up a continuing buying relationship to make it pay. To just continually give costly free stuff free is stupid.

Easy does it!

Easy Stuff Can Backfire

It needs to be said there is a dark side to this easy tech running our lives. Easy can go wrong. Business owners are advised to beware of Darth Vader taking the force back. Say your Internet goes, for example, or network crashes. These are nightmares at the worst time and get expensive. Ours were down recently and, simultaneously, two main admin workers were out of town. I still had my receptionist so I reminded her to make a bank deposit with the scanner machine but she did not know how. Me either. I thought we can still do it the old fashioned way as I rustled for deposit slips. We filled them out and she went to the bank while I covered. Then a delivery came needing a check, which are generated by the computer. We both looked at each other. I asked the delivery guy to return while I searched for paper checks. I found them and asked Kelly to fill one out. "We still need the signature stamp Cindy uses, Tom" said Kelly. "No wait, I can sign it for real Kelly." I think an owner has to be able to go to "manual mode" should a shutdown take away his easy.

I experienced a nightmare of easy backfiring while on vacation. My wife's new car has the key fob, again, saving the sweating of using a real key. It has to be inside the car for the starter button to start the car. She carries it in her purse and loves it since she never has to find her key much less turn one. This convenient fob thing first got me in trouble when I went to use her car and thus took her purse too since the key was in it and I was not about to try and fathom its whereabouts deep in its recesses. Naturally, while gone, she needed something out of her purse.

Another backfire came when I dropped her at Burger King and drove down the street to fill up. Once fueled, I could not restart the car! No fob with me so no engine restart as cars cued behind me. I frantically looked in the manual, surely for some way to quickly get going but there was none. There was, not making this up, 21 pages on the key fob, (21 pages!), but nothing pertinent. I called her, explained, and she walked toward the station. She and my daughter gathered up bags of burgers and began the trek to bring me the sacred fob. I asked one car for a ride and they rolled up their window. A pickup truck guy said sure to a lift and we plucked my wife, daughter and bag of cold burgers from the roadside. In the words of the truck driver "sometimes too much technology is not a good thing bro". Amen. What if it had been my daughter dropping my wife at the airport as she flew off with said fob?

Here is another. Did you know if you put a hotel card key, another convenience to eliminate keys, into the same pocket as an iPhone, it erases the card key possibly leaving you stranded at the door of your room at a critical moment. The easy effort of getting rid of keys seems to bring new *inconveniences*. Then there was the time my daughter jammed up the proceedings at a Red Box as she could not get the machine to accept her return DVD which turned out to be one she owned. Buyer beware. Technology giveth and technology taketh. Is there not real danger letting the chips and software remove us too far from reality?

Now you understand how easy things really are in business. Let's move on to see if you can land customers and sell your stuff.

Moe's summation: " I get the easy theme. I find that if something is made easy it happens more often. For example, when I want a stomach rub I trek over to my owner's feet, and any visitor's as well, flop on my back and, bingo, I get the rub."

3 Someone Can Sell

Y ou may say you are in the computer business, food business, car business, software development business, electric business or whatever business, but before that, you are in the sales business. Before you can do what you 'do' you have to sell to somebody or not be able to do what you do. The number one need of any small business is revenue generation meaning you have to sell your stuff.

You will have to know how to do so to progress. Say you have a great product or service. Several employees are technically able to fix anything. Your support help is eager and wonderful. You have advertised but disappointed at results and cost. There has been coverage of your company in local papers. You have participated in networking groups. You represent a fine product with name recognition. All fine.

Yet, things are stagnant and new business lacking. You can be the smartest owner in the world but you still need someone to go face to face with customers to obtain business! That is the work of a sales person. I well remember this example in IBM sales school. It is said "build a better mouse trap and the world will beat a path to your door." An inventor did, a jaw type thing you could reuse and empty out the dead mouse without touching it. He received a patent but the company failed because nobody could sell and not many came to the door. They said a better slogan would be "build a better mouse trap and have salespeople beat a path to the customer's door."

Businesses have a lot of needs but none greater than obtaining more business which is the work of salespeople. Having sales ability on board should be an idea that comes before your business idea. I cannot think of a more important entrepreneurial skill for business building or for holding on to one. It is a skill that lets you be more in control of your business building. Business ownership is a ground pounding doing thing more than an idea thing and nothing exemplifies that like outbound sales work. Doing more business means somebody doing business and that is the salesperson.

Even if your company is the world's greatest marketing machine, has high SEO, awesome web presence, meets and tweets, conducts social media campaigns, and uses direct mail, all getting traffic, what good is that if once prospects come there are no sales people to close deals? Marketing and advertising need to be *in support of* the salespeople and *not in place of* them.

Coming even before selling customers is selling your employees. You have to be able to convince them of the merits of your company, your products and your service to your level of belief. They will then carry this passion into the marketplace. It is OK if your eyes and veins bulge as you are convincing them. Also be there to shore up any doubts that may come about in these areas.

To succeed your business must have sales capability. It is so important it is our longest chapter.

"Before you can do what you 'do' you have to be able to sell. Same if you want to continue to do what you do."

You can't be a successful business owner without knowing sales and selling some yourself. It is a big part of the job. Responsibility for producing revenue is a prime responsibility of ownership that can never be relinquished. It is how cash moves from warehouse to checkbook. It's called making a sale and it is exciting. Small business success is sales driven. Whether it is yourself as sales ninja or hiring good salespeople and a sales manager, there is no higher priority. Indeed, if you are a company under 15 about half of your time should be spent selling!

Sales are as critical to a business as touchdowns to a football team. Show me the most successful companies and I will show you those with the best salespeople. Selling more stuff cures most business ills including the number one business problem of not having enough business. You want more working capital? Sell more stuff. You want more bottom line? Sell more stuff. You want a bigger company? Sell more stuff. If you can hire good sales people you will not have to go begging for funding because you create it. I would take a squadron of high performing sales reps over a slick marketing campaign or more funding any day.

A question owners get is "What are your sales?" On your income statement is that big category entitled Sales. To fill it you need salespeople. Sales people are the athletes if not Special Forces of business. They live with uncertainty, engage in competitive combat, endure the most difficulty, overcome the most adversity and make the biggest difference. Did I mention they have idiosyncrasies? But alas, these people make the business world go 'round. And when I say salesperson I mean an outside salesperson. Inside salespeople sell, yes, but take little responsibility for obtaining prospects.

Real Salespeople Defined

In outside sales the salesperson finds the business and with inside sales the business finds the salesperson. That said, the dynamics of the salesperson are changing. The Bureau of Labor Statistics says there are about 15 million salespeople but there has been a decrease from Internet sales. Internet sales have reduced primarily commodity hard goods sales jobs that went to mostly inside salespeople. Some outside salespeople are moving inside but using outbound sales methods using computers and software. They work inside a building, yes, but use techniques similar to the outside salesperson.

It may develop that everyone will be labeled a salesperson and all utilize outside salesperson techniques. In any case, as we shall see and you may have heard, real salespeople do not sell anything. *They solve problems and are paid to do so.* They convey a product, knowledge, a procedure, some software or a human (or combination of those) to do this. We know there are always plenty of problems needing attention in B2B or B2C which is why there will always be a need for real salespeople.

Sales work is the business end of business, the tip of the spear. It brings the end zone or the ozone. It is not to be confused with marketing. Marketing helps set the table for salespeople, hopefully brings warm prospects, but is not the business of actually selling something. That requires another specialist—the salesperson—one of your most valuable employees. You may design marketing campaigns, social media efforts and web page tactics, all in hopes of acquiring customers to avoid the more successful, but stressful effort of employing sales people. You may even seek venture capital to fund your efforts instead of making sales calls. Big mistake most likely. Do both.

While seeking funds, funding, and something easy, your competition is kicking you by hiring salespeople who are talking to prospects about buying things and they are getting orders. Hire a good salesperson for God's sake, who should be the sharpest tool in your shed and possess creative instincts that sniff out and close business. They are the hunters and they enjoy it. Do you remember any history about the earliest humans and how tribes were divided by the hunter-gatherers and the farmers to survive? We are still like that and the hunter-gatherers were our first outside salespeople. Sales types are a bit prickly, complain some, but like the thrill of the hunt. To one that can meet these criteria sales work brings an above average six figure income in a good year.

If you cannot do it then hire someone but good ones are hard to find. You need sales experience yourself to supervise sales work because you must know it to deal with it. Tending to salespeople is high maintenance. This work and degree of difficulty is just this side of herding airborne geese. As challenging as Bill O'Reilly moderating The View. But only when sales are lost or quota not met. There is great fun and camaraderie among sales types and nothing is more exciting than when things are moving, sales closing, and quotas being met.

The Sales Persona

There is no one more valuable to a small business than a person who sells but it takes something extra to understand this species. America's needs move by truck but who fills them? Salespeople. Nothing would halt commerce quicker than salespeople striking. God bless these self starting, self winding, Energizer Bunnies who get knocked down but get back up and usually, not always by any means, with enthusiasm. They start every month at zero but are pretty sure they have a nationwide sale to General Electric in their back pocket.

That is optimism to have as an owner too. Owners find themselves sympathizing with their eccentric salesperson even if, simultaneously, looking forward to justifying firing the son of a gun. Admin types are rarely fond of salespeople who they perceive have large egos, poor with paperwork that messes up their day, being overpaid, and somewhat untrustworthy. Salespeople are not that happy with admins either labeling them the sales prevention unit. It would not be unusual for a hard charging sales rep to feel he should be running the company and he certainly feels superior to those that do. Now, now, boys and girls, can we all just get along......? Well maybe.

To cure this gee haw remind that no salespeople means no revenue means no jobs. Lay out the dictum *"everyone* is in sales." The simplest way to accomplish that is to have "always be asking" as the sales mantra of non-salespeople. It is possible admin people have more customer contacts in a week than salespeople.

Looking inside the sales brain you see a Willy Wonka factory with Ooompa Loompas scurrying about pulling a sales creation together or a Hadron Particle Collider in full collision mode. The sales mind is the eighth wonder and can't be cloned. It may take an algorithm written by Bill Gates just to get a grip on it. This brain allocates time each month to worrying. Will my customer pass credit? Will my product cause cancer? Will my competitor cut the price to ridiculous? Will my customer call in sick the day we are to close? Will the demo machine break down? Will my quota be raised? Will I be fired? Yes to all these sometimes.

Sales types walk between raindrops trying to keep negativity from landing and need constant praise, recognition, inspiration and reassurance to counter living with the considerable uncertainty. Then comes the euphoria when it pulls together and sales happen. Feels like a gain in the market, sinking a birdie putt, a slot machine payout, bagging a big deer or taking delivery of a new car. Yes, it can be another sort of bi-polar existence but if you stay ahead of the game sales is the greatest job there is.

Salespeople are quasi-business owners and business owners quasi-salespeople. Both are salepreneuers which are those who sell to build a business. Of the 28 million small businesses only 250,000 are manufacturers so the small business theater is dominated by salepreneurs, technicians and customer service people. Salespeople are as close as you come to being in business for yourself yet still using another's money. They get paid more if they sell more, less if they don't. They love the freedom and the open ended pay but are not crazy about all the uncertainties—like the owner.

Finding good salespeople is difficult—one of your hardest hires. The best are those you train from scratch. I had such a person answer an ad. She arrived in a banger of a car wearing a loud suit coat with huge lapels. I hurried the interview knowing this was not someone I recognized as a professional sales rep. I will not prolong this but she called back several times and returned four other times without an appointment. The fourth time I realized these are qualities you cannot teach, persistence and tenacity. I hired her at low pay plus commission. She sold for 15 years, became my VP and partner in another business. You never know how someone will work out, but if you see persistence, tenacity and no give-up, all un- teachable prized qualities, the student has presented!

Yes, You Must Prospect

Let's move to the work of selling something. Sales success works off this formula:

Sales Calls + Presentations = Sales.

Sales calls, meaning cold calling or prospecting, is everyone's least favorite thing to do. If you will not prospect, or have call reluctance, find other work. Prospecting is the original form of networking. Call it hot knocking if you like, because each call puts you closer to the law of averages turning in your favor and landing a warm one! To attain your monthly sales quota you will need three times that amount in working business in your sales funnel.

When I began building my business I was frequently in salepreneur mode making as many prospecting calls as the workday would allow. I knew what was at stake and that it was on me like I wanted. I got irritated when the lunch hour arrived. When I looked at the metro size of Memphis, and my considerable determination to canvass it, I realized it was bigger than I could ever cover. Yay! More business to find than I can get to, was my thought. Top sales makers are not any smarter or talented than others but work like someone is coming to repossess their business.

Whether over the phone, in person, by email or all three, there must be continual prospecting to make sales. If you will not prospect regularly you soon are hungry and jobless. I see people enter sales work and when asked how it is going say " I am busy getting the word out." Right. Can be good work there but hopefully they also are "getting the lead out." Sales work requires above average physical fitness to maintain the sheer number of calls combined with high levels of intensity and enthusiasm. A good sign is reps wearing out more shoe leather than chair fabric or mouse pads. You rarely see a successful outside sales rep that is overweight.

Some prefer the electronic phone-it-in mentality to personal sales work thinking that by getting their name out, a Facebook page, website, SEO, Twitter followers and cloaking themselves in tech they will get orders upon opening their email. This mentality may be a carryover from dot.com which, remember, produced the dot.com bust. Trying to electronically outsource the heavy lifting of sales work and finesse it is like sweet talking a lion with, "Here kitty, kitty." Good luck. Techno heads need to spend as much time staring at people as their screens.

This generation of "no, I don't answer the phone" business people, depending too much on digital metrics to define success as well as attain it, are distancing themselves from decision makers in the process. People skills diminish with this digital distancing. Most business is still closed face to face or based upon a relationship with the customer and not with our devices. Our alphabet is being replaced with a textabet.

Moe Lesson

For useful metaphors I look at my dog Moe and see what he is teaching. Moe sets a great example for prospectors. He digs constantly and the yard is full of trenches. Moe first sniffs over the ground, zeros in on his spots undeterred, and never stops the digging. Bingo! We have another Moe Lesson. Sales reps need to do similar, always digging, digging, digging and looking for the opportunities. You have to enjoy that process for where it leads. Moe still does his daily digging so best be as persistent to succeed. Enjoy the digging. I'll give an example of this Moe Lesson. I don't prospect but will dig if it looks promising. While at Nike NFL I overheard "Joe is at Nike Golf." In years of having this account I never heard of Nike Golf and was told it was just five people. I knew Nike does not do anything small, got the address, and went.

Sign said Menlo Logistics with hundreds of cars in the lot. I asked the guard about Nike Golf. "This is it, " he said. It was the only location

Nike sub-contracted. Further digging found the five and the other 300 working in the 500,000 square feet were Menlo. I sell warehouse products and a great sales opportunity presented itself. You only uncover these opportunities prospecting in person, digging, looking, and asking and by being there. Another example of the power of *eyeball reconnaissance* came from my asking for a tour of a company I could not get into otherwise, for the purpose of viewing their products. The manager toured us and I noticed many water jug stations. "Wow," I said. "We have a product to stop jug usage. Would you be interested?" I asked. "I hate those ," he replied. This would not have been possible from a phone inquiry or other sales effort other than eyeball reconnaissance.

Prospect intelligently. Most cities have Book of Lists of the top 25 businesses in every category or the Top 100 private businesses. Buy a current list from Info USA or Sales Genie that are target markets and call it. Build an email contact list. Be guided by famous bank robber Willie Sutton, who, after robbing many banks was caught. Asked why he robbed banks his response was "Because that's where the money is." It's the same for you. Call on the largest accounts you know can use your product because that is where the money is.

Prospecting vs. Cold Calling

The terms prospecting and cold calling are not that interchangeable. Prospecting includes some cold calling but the majority effort is directed at existing customers which makes it warmer. Pure cold calling is used when you have no customers or must find more. Prospecting means you re-visit customers you have done business with but maybe not for a while. They are familiar with you and have bought something previously. These calls take the form of " it's time for new one" ,or, you are seeking to sell them an entirely different product. Since *Small Business Survival 101* is primarily for existing business it assumes you have a base. Most salespeople will not stay long if hired for 100% cold calling. Whether sales rep or business owner, more success is found seeking business opportunities—outbound selling—rather than hoping they find you.

Keep a keen eye on prospecting activities. Monitor them and have activity recorded into CRM, customer relationship management software. CRM, like Salesforce or Goldmine, allows supervisors to view activity and records it. Should the employee leave you have the records and the new rep picks up with them. These records are company property and not the employee's. Even very good salespeople need pushing to increase prospecting but if too much urging is required it is time for a new salesperson. This importance of documenting prospecting, or any important activity, lets me take this moment to again remind: *you can only expect from what you inspect!* Check the prospecting data regularly to insure it will support life! If not, raise hell.

The more success at closing sales the more interested a rep gets in prospecting because he realizes each call means moving closer to a sale. He is a quarterback taking beating after beating to reach the end zone and happily gets back up, lured by pay dirt. It is the work of being a quarterback and prospecting is the work of a rep. Unless your rep is straight commission his salary is for making prospecting calls and product demonstrations. It is not appearance money or a retainer but a *production salary* and should be referred to as such. It takes a strong partnership between owner and rep to make each other successful.

Ultimately, the sales person's job is to move prospects to the point of closing business—to be a 'mover and a shaker.' Prospects have other things to do and will tell you so. Of course you do not push but you must nudge and be comfortable with that. You will use professional persistence and not be easily deterred. There are those who can and those who won't. My wife gets asked to call on businesses to raise money for a few charities by selling tickets and the like. She would go out and come home and say "I just cannot do this. I cannot ask people to buy anything. I don't see how you do this?"

I have come across some owners who believe you are not supposed to call on a business. I asked one how he got new customers and he answered "word of mouth." You may get some business like that but certainly not enough. "Do you make sales calls?" I asked. "Well, no, you see signs on buildings that say no soliciting so......," which explains why he only has two employees. Those signs are there but generally do not mean professional reps that come through the front door of a business open to the public. Sure, you may get turned away—it's part of it—but 90% of the time not because of a no soliciting sign. You at least obtained the name of the contact person and will try to set up an appointment. Ironically, web heads get turned away, too, by being spammed, blocked or horrors, de-friended.

A Good Sales Call

If you prospect enough you eventually speak to prospective buyers, which is about the approach call. It better be good. Its basics mean you and customer talk equally. The more the customer talks, the better. If you dominate may as well terminate it because it means the customer is not interested. It is more interesting to your prospects to *be shown*, rather than told. Show a clip, printed material, reference letter, customer list, or the product itself in a demonstration. Showing is better than talking.

Ask open-ended questions that uncover customer needs and get him talking in lengthy sentences. Do this by asking questions starting with "W's and the "H"—What, When, Where, Why, How. They require answering in sentences instead of one word like yes or no which are typical answers in a closed-ended question that do not take you far. You uncover the needs as the customer answers. "What are your profit responsibilities? What problems stand in your way? When do you plan to expand? Where do you see the company in six months? Why have you not upgraded your technology? How do you plan to increase profits? How do you feel about that?"

Closed ended questions help at times like, "Are you satisfied with your current service?" If answered 'no' then follow with, 'Why?' to judge customer sentiment toward competitors. I find asking two 'why?' questions back to back is particularly effective. Once you uncovered the needs, ask the "If I could ... would you be interested?" question. "If I could solve these problems, would you be interested in buying my product?" Getting an affirmative is the customer's green light, and then you show how you solve.

There are two methods to obtain responses favorable enough to keep a prospect moving. Demonstrating that you sell something that satisfies needs or solves a problem, as just discussed, is the most effective and called the *need/satisfaction* method. The other method is *stimulus response* and mostly a form of promotion used in retail or commodity selling. The stimulus response salesperson says "We have 30% off this week on widgets providing you spend $1000. This is a limited time offer and satisfaction is guaranteed." Hopefully customers respond 'yes' to this stimulation and spend $1000.

Need/ satisfaction takes longer requiring time to uncover specific problems for which you sell solutions. For example, if you are a real estate salesperson a golden moment is "John, find a sublease for my space and I'll buy the building from you." You have a sale if you solve the problem of finding a renter. John finds the need, satisfies it by finding a renter, and gets a sale. The salesperson primarily drives stimulus response while need/satisfaction is led by listening and questioning the customer and more driven by him. In need satisfaction customers usually have multiple needs: "your product must be faster, easier to use, smaller in size, come in green and be cheaper." These become the buying criteria to satisfy to make a sale. Need satisfaction is the selling method for non-commodity products.

Push The Pain

There is a critical step in need/satisfaction that guides you and the customer to uncover needs the company doesn't know it has. This skill turns "we're fine," customers into buyers. I cannot emphasize its importance. It is a skill mastered by top reps that turns things your way where there seemingly was no way. It goes by a few terms. At my school it was, "Upsetting the customer's homeostasis," translated, "The state of the human." Others call it, "pushing the pain."

The goal is making the customer realize something is not fine, which makes him uncomfortable, feeling pain and thus motivated to see it your way and buy. This technique is an excellent way to change another's thinking. Buyers are focused on some things over others or overlook others. That's normal; we are all a bit ADHD. In these overlooked areas business problems brew that savvy reps spot and hope to make the customers aware. Let's take three examples.

The example used in sales school was the band uniform salesman in *The Music Man*. He was prospecting in a city that had too much juvenile delinquency. He presented this to the school board and this presentation is immortalized in the "I tell ya, ya got trouble, trouble, and that's trouble with a capital T. You have trouble, I say trouble, here in River City!" Without prolonging this there was trouble with juveniles because they were idle after school and if the school started a band this would reduce delinquency. If they agreed then, of course, they buy his band uniforms and instruments. Thus the music man took the juvenile delinquency statistics, painstakingly showed the problems they represented, and made everyone realize the pain going with the teens.

They were persuaded of a solution which was buying his band outfits. Another example, as we dig deeper. There is the Happy Potty app touting where the cleanest restrooms are. Sure, everyone likes clean over dirty but that may not be enough to change routes thus losing sales. To better articulate pain points they identify all restroom germs and illnesses they cause. Then, armed with this Dick Tracy work, ask open ended, pain-producing questions: "Were you aware unclean restrooms contain e-coli which causes severe nausea and the staph virus which causes infections? How do you feel about exposing your children? Would you like a way to avoid this risk?" So by posing these questions you produced pain motivation and hopefully a sale.

One last example since this technique is that important. My company sells a water unit that uses water coming into a building and replaces water jug units. Jug units are transported, made of plastic, have to be changed, re-ordered and re-delivered by a diesel belching truck. My rep: "Why buy water when it comes into your building nearly free? I read you have a green initiative. Do you see how un-green water jug buying is? How does everyone feel about changing them?" The rep then asks "If I could show a better way, would you be interested?" Try to produce three pain points and give each a bit to sink in and allow time for a customer response. Your silence is golden here. This technique moves thinking off disinterested to interested.

Seen the recent Batman movie? Did they upset the status quo of Batman fans or what? There are numerous pain points. Batman has taken a beating, is literally on his back, is broke, the bad guy outsmarted him, lost his girl, he limps, is depressed, fires his butler, walks with a cane, has not played with his gadgets for years and is left for dead in a prison. Stop now please. Give the Batman-beat-down-of-the bad- guys-solution we crave. We are so ready to buy it to relieve such pain. All which leaves the producers yelling SOLD!

You might say that selling is solving. That is what it needs to be for today's high earner. It is not so much about the product as about the solve. Companies will always have business problems to solve.

Strong Benefit Statements Needed

Do not waste valuable time in a sales call yakking football or fishing. Customers have time limits, even if you don't, so don't waste it talking trivia. This means more time to discuss the supporting research from your surveying and for demonstrating the product and its problem solving benefit statements. They are what the customer is buying.

Giving great benefit statements is hard. Even experienced reps think they are doing so only to fall short. Sales 101 teaches when selling state product Features, its Functions, then its Benefits—FFB in the sales world. A trainee might say "here is the copier's reduction button and it shrinks images 6% to 80% and stop. That is stating feature (reduction button), function (reduce image) but the benefit statement, the important part, is left off.

Stating benefits is where real salespeople separate from amateurs. It is the kind of statement a lawyer makes in court that turns the tide. In my example the statement should be "therefore this reducing feature eliminates cumbersome, expensive, and oversize binders and their larger file cabinets that waste time and slow response to customers." Another example is selling a light bulb. Most would say "here is a light bulb (feature) and it brings light (function)."

Many stop there but a benefit statement continues: "therefore you can return to enjoying sewing, reading your book, avoid tripping over things, injuring yourself and needing a doctor." An ad in our paper said "The Sounds of Summer Are Returning." I thought of a singing group but it was the lead benefit statement for a hearing aid. It never mentioned 'now you can hear'. A stick of Old Spice deodorant takes the prize: "If your grandfather hadn't worn it, you wouldn't exist." This is verbatim and not the usual '24 hour protection' function statement.

Actually, your bathroom countertop is a good place to look for schooling in benefit statements. Manufacturers battle in this multi-billion dollar market to win space on your countertop. Their huge marketing budgets have the best benefit statements money can buy. A favorite of mine is some stuff for women called Night Repair. What better benefit to a woman than to get her face worked on while sleeping!

Benefits Make Them Buy

It is the benefit statement that triggers a buy. The thing is, most products have multiple benefits and some the buyer has not thought about. For example, take a simple shovel. Its benefits are that it can dig a hole easier than by hand. Simple enough. But it can also be used to scrap, stab weeds, knock down dirt dobber nests, kill a snake, measure something or hold open a door. You could benefit from one if you never dug a hole. So if I am a shovel salesman I make sure I know all this and listen carefully to my prospect to see if he has any of these needs to fill that he didn't realize could be done by a shovel. There is a sales technique about this called The Ben Franklin. Yes, that Ben. He found that the seller who piles up the biggest number of benefits gets the business.

Uncovering these benefits is a much harder task for the Internet to do than an attentive sales rep. To ensure you issue a benefit statement, after giving the feature / function, say "therefore" to lead into it. Another way to do this is answering "So what?" If you make a strong benefit statement they will never ask.

Uncovering the particular needs of a customer, their pain points, and solving them is what professional salesmanship does. If you are a pure product salesperson you spend your time pointing to the product and showing what it does. Professional sales reps spend their time listening to customer needs and researching their problems. Frequently the sales rep sees these problems before the customer. This is not because the customer is stupid he is just not focused on the topic. Accurately surmising customer problems before the customer does is a skill of high earning pros. The rep doing the best investigation, the Dick Tracy work, who best understands the company's issues, obtains the advantage.

I instruct reps to interview as many employees as allowed to gain decisive insights. At closing, it is powerful to be able to say: "Mary in accounting stressed the new machine do A, B, and C, and hopefully D since D would save valuable time. Our machine does wonderfully with D." When conducting a needs analysis stand under the biggest umbrella with that umbrella representing the company's main goals. You are safe assuming some are general like "increase employee productivity," or "decrease customer response time " or, of course, "save money" to address. You want these goals to be ones articulated by the highest company authority, maybe found in the company's annual report, mission statement or web site, then state how your product, even obliquely, helps.

But again, never assume the customer gets what you are saying. They need it stated even if obvious to you. They think about many other things in a day than your product and all you think about is your product. State it! Great benefit statements, along with the research behind them, prevent sales from deteriorating into price battles. If a customer discerns no difference in benefits between competitors then price decides.

To reduce price battles ask the customer to prioritize each buying criterion to know buying priorities. Price will usually be one of them but probably not number one. Prioritizing the buying criteria is important. This means the customer states, say, four things, ranked one through four in importance in determining how he decides. Once established they help shield you from minor factors, the tail wagging the dog stuff, that suddenly decides things out of nowhere. "Sir, why would the landscaping decide things when you never mentioned it and said the number one thing is the new space must include a large warehouse?" My son, who sold equipment for me, called these unexpected changes "X" factors. "Why did we lose Park?" I would ask. "X factors Dad. Stuff came out of nowhere that went against us." Prioritizing the buying criteria and gaining the customer's agreement on them can reduce surprises. Another preventative is asking each time you meet if anything has changed since you last met.

Adding Value

People pay more for things benefiting their needs, adding value to their lives, and just as much for *perceived* benefits. Never neglect the power of perceived benefits even though concrete ones are better. People buy gas at Kroger because they perceive a discount with their Kroger card even though they may be paying more for groceries. You may spray Lysol believing it kills every germ, keeping your family healthy, for which you willingly pay extra. At my car wash a sign says "A clean car rides better." Once in your head you feel it is true. Dresses of a certain style are touted as 'slimming.' Of course the dress did not come with weight loss but if customers *perceive* they look thinner then SOLD! You pick your babysitter, not on who charges least, but on who you perceive keeps your children safest, and willing pay more. Selling well means making people feel well.

I was grabbing a spray product off the grocery shelf when a competing one had a newly designed bottle boasting "Sprays to the last drop!" It had a clever window in the container bottom showing where the last drop lived so when it was gone you know you sprayed it. Now the monetary value of the last drop, or even the last few drops, has to be what, two cents? *Hardly the point!* You got it all! It makes you feel good! You perceive a great benefit here which is enjoying a victory. And they sell more spray. The spraying people are trying to poach the last-bit-of-toothpaste people who squeeze to the end too (you know who you are). Again, two cents worth of product value but manufacturers know the customer *perceives* this as a satisfying victory and feels good about it. That is all that matters. Cha ching. Another marketing lesson from the bathroom.

When I worked at a department store I learned women's cosmetics had the highest profit percentage of anything in the store. Why? Because women wanted the perceived value added to their appearance from using the new concoction. Women put on a new cream of some kind and say to themselves: "I am more beautiful, look younger, smell good, glow, and thus I am now more desirable." That is a lot of benefit coming out of a small tube so it is sold, whether the benefits are true or not no matter the price. Perception really is reality in sales so pay attention to customer perceptions. Benefits pay. Benefits sell. Match benefit statements to needs. Satisfy the need. Uncover the need. Do your Dick Tracy work. Be needy.

When you do this you do what a business must to thrive: ADD VALUE to its products and services. It is where you whip the big box stores. Sell products that benefit customers by adding values of expertise, instruction, implementation, convenience and reassurance on how the product is best deployed. Products and services that do not require such additional support, like a piece of self explanatory hardware, are commodities without substantial profit which makes your company weak. You may carry some commodities but prosperity comes from adding value not commodity. For example, my company sells medical software. There is a license fee with 40% margin. There is a larger charge for training and implementation to help the doctor make the transition to the EMR. This adds a great value to the doctor and my business.

My son has a sales position with Synthes who makes expensive hardware sold to surgeons to mend broken bones. The company is constantly improving their plates, screws and rods for which ongoing sales training is held. Parker's job is to get time with the physician and show the benefits of the new stuff for which he hopes to get a sale. His efforts add value to his products and to the physician's understanding. This too, sets up a continuing and ongoing relationship with the customer which is the kind of selling you want to do.

Another example of a value-added, problem-solving sales rep is the packaging salesperson. These reps know customers have products always changing in size, weight and quantity. A new product may require a more protective package or one that displays the product more or one that holds more or all three. Another may need to be waterproof or be able to be stacked. The kind of material, its color, shape and strength to be the right package takes collaboration between customer and salesman to arrive at the right combination and thus lead to good sale. Finding this solution provides considerable benefit for the customer.

I like to buy custom made suits and shirts. They just fit better and last longer making me enjoy them more, all added value to me. I could buy something off the rack but prefer the custom stuff which requires a tailor to become involved and help me buy something that melds together my specifications. This adds value to my clothes and adds value to his business at the same time. The packaging salesperson, and my tailor, are not providing "off the rack" solutions so they are not vulnerable to being Googled or challenged by the Internet. As a business or as a sales rep sell more custom solutions than off-the-rack ones.

Practice/Train

Owners are quick to shout to their salesperson "just get the business" with scant thought to profitability. They would find a better pay off if they would turn the yelling to themselves saying "train the salespeople better." A more knowledgeable salesperson is a more profitable salesperson.

Sales technique needs to be practiced to keep them sharp. Do this by role-playing, someone being the customer and someone else the sales rep. Use your office manager or service manager to make semi-real practice sales calls on during a sales meeting or when new products rolls out. Sometimes a customer will agree to do this for real at a sales meeting. I used to have a few decision makers come to sales meetings, help us train, and give their perceptions of us and competitors—what each company did well and not so well. Try it. Maybe you can role-play at home with a spouse.

The act of selling is like any skill and requires practice to keep it sharp. It is one of the most vital abilities you company must have to succeed so don't leave it to chance. You can be sure your opponents practice.

Self Discipline Required

Successful sales work is about discipline. Owners have to demand it or won't get it, and sales suffer. We remember from childhood that discipline is nobody's favorite and means requiring things we want an easier way to do! Or don't want to do. Reps need constant reminders, recognition, motivation and praise to stay disciplined similar to professional athletes. I enjoy putting up signs like No *Typing at 2:00!*, *Making Quota Pardons All Sin!*, *No Whining!*, *No Excuses!*, *Let Pride Decide! Make Another Call!* Both salespeople and athletes have in common performing at peak as long as possible to get results. Sales work is a numbers game you work *tirelessly* until the law of averages tilts your way.

You begin and the sales universe is a wide funnel narrowing towards fewer buyers. How many buyers depends upon how far your discipline takes you in number of calls and presentations. In excellent time management. In staying current on product knowledge. It is the "how bad you want it?" thing we ask of athletes. I require salespeople be at their first call at 9:00 and stay out until 11:30. From 1:00 until 4:30 they are back in the field. These are the only hours anyone will see you. That is game time and no time to be in the locker room where you can't score. IBM brass got on us if we lingered: "Pease, I don't see any customers to call on. Why are you here?" The answer is I am unorganized and undisciplined, sir. There is a lot of freedom in sales work, one of its attractions. Freedom is a factor in why you chose your own business, too, so you understand its appeal and its distractions. This freedom can become a time vampire that buries time squanderers.

Find reasons to make more calls. It is not in your control what customers do but always in your control to make sales calls. You do need to be a rocket scientist to make sales calls because rocket science is about propulsion and propulsion is about overcoming inertia and overcoming inertia is about making those calls. best discipline themselves to overcome any sales activity inertia. To maximize valuable customer face time do prep work at home. Proposals, calculations, power points, email drafts, and the like, need to be done after hours. Not much different from, say, an athlete working out or studying the playbook so he is all in at game time. That is how you position to win.

A disciplined rep that works a full day every day (imagine) will win his share and beat more established reps that pick and choose prospects and do not make as many calls. If not making calls, in one form or another, all day long you have no right to expect a booming business. Most reps know most companies are not going to buy from them right now. But they soldier on until they find some that do, maybe 5-10 for the month. Worth it!

Making sales is hard work and takes skill. The more skilled you are the fewer mistakes made and the more business you close. The sales process is a fragile one and such that hardly any mistakes are allowed or you are out. Sales is a profession like being a doctor, pilot or an electrician. It means you are professional at something which means you do the very same thorough, step-by-step methodology every time no matter what the conditions. This produces the highest results and fewest errors. Seasoned reps whip rookies nearly every time, and their closing rate is higher, because they know how to avoid mistakes. I think some businesses and owners never move past amateur status in sales and that hurts. When I started at IBM, considered to have the best salespeople, they would not let you into the field without three months of training. That is how seriously they take it. Get training from a pro. Understand the methods and the mistakes.

Show Don't Tell

A big part of selling successfully is *showing* what your product does rather than telling. Telling is not selling. Maximum talking goal is 50% with the customer talking the other half. People tune out if you talk too much. Do you remember kindergarten Show and Tell? You talked about your new Transformer and the kids yawned. When you pulled it from your pocket they were mesmerized. We are still like that. We want to be shown because we have shorter attention spans than ever, maybe shorter than in kindergarten. We tweet 140 characters, multi-task, use weird abbreviations, vote based upon sound bites or 20 second clips of gaffes. It's how people make decisions these days. It's where we are so showing is more important than ever.

While sales training in the IBM branch office the trainer gave me a lesson on this. I was demonstrating the Correcting Selectric typewriter and knew everything about it. I was to demonstrate it to the trainer. I spouted every feature function and benefit for fifteen minutes and I was pleased. "This is a demonstration, not a presentation," commented the trainer. He pointed to the paper in the typewriter on which I had typed only five characters. "People watching a new typewriter demonstration expect to see it type. Next time I want 100 characters on that paper." Whatever you are waltzing make sure it is dancing!

So show it more than tell it. Act out. Use props. I was at a regional session to train reps in techniques on a new machine. There is nothing harder than selling salespeople. The new copiers had duplexing and to justify its cost reps showed money saved using both sides of paper. Most reps were not impressed with the savings. Time for show and tell. I held up a 50 page report that was now 25 and wrote what the savings were if mailed. I showed savings from buying filing cabinets if this report were filed. I showed time saved from flipping 25 less pages. For the coup I took just one ream of 500 sheets and threw it all over the room like confetti as it blanketed the floor. "That, gentlemen, is 500 less pieces of paper flowing throw companies creating a mess like this not to mention the time handling each. Enough said?" It was. The showing sold them, not the talking.

An object which serves as a metaphor creates mental images, and shows the point clearer than words, and is remembered longer, so use pictures, videos, and You Tubes. Put the product in the customer's hand. Showing means conducting a product demonstration directed at customer needs. The customer participates which breaks tension and focuses their attention. The demonstration shows how the product meets the customer's buying criteria like its speed, the ease of using it, the quality of it, the reliability of it and the versatility of it. Then the price of it.

These points are universal buying criteria and how most customers evaluate purchases. If you direct demonstrations to them, show how your product best meets or exceeds these expectations, and any others the customer mentioned, you close a sale.

A trial period may be next. Trials are excellent Trojan Horses to gain engagement with a customer. If a trial is installed visit it daily, however briefly, because people do not absorb everything in one instruction session. They can hate your machine in one day if its unfamiliarity frustrates them. Another caveat—a product trial may give rise to new questions, or produce more customer research, so always ask: "Has anything changed?" It likely has, maybe in your favor, maybe not. Generally, customers respect your effort of giving them a trial, which puts your product where your mouth is.

Owners have an advantage over mere salespeople when selling which is the power to win on "Ts and Cs", Terms and Conditions. You can change them on the spot. You may extend 90 days free or grant an option at 6 months to cancel or allow free use of product B if you buy product A. Winning on terms and conditions is helpful when a competitor is selling the same product and prices are equal. They can keep you from having to lower the price.

Cook Proposals, Then Cool

At some point you write proposals. The discipline in doing this is pivotal to its profitability. Proposals are worked happily and the mental picture is bagging a deal and how great that will be. In a bit of euphoric state you offer free this, free that, 25% off this, 30% off that and a free trip around the world if you buy today! Phew! That should get it. Question is, will it be worth it? Here is a tip that has made me tens of thousands over my career. Do all the above, in full lather, but let the proposal cool a day or two and *then* finalize it. Remove at least one free thing and one discount. You can do it. These need not be huge but at least something is the point. Then give the proposal to the customer. Let this be a discipline that counters giving away the store. It saves significant profits and causes few lost deals.

The brain works best when given space. I have published over 100 weekly columns on small business and each takes three hours. However, I always take five days to complete one as the draft cools. Each day new thoughts enter that make the column better. Writing is a lot of mental work, as is selling, and when the brain is weary it does not do its best work. I advise anyone writing a book to take twelve months. You may complete it in six but additional months of reflection, letting things cool, and the opportunity to use hindsight, are priceless. So it is with business proposals. Do not hurry it because that is usually expensive, incomplete and not your best moment. Get the emotion and fatigue out of it.

Tip: when preparing any proposal give the customer choices. Buyers like choices. Give your recommendation and then an upgrade from it as well as a downgrade for a total of three. If the customer feels they have choices it can keep them from shopping around.

Why People Buy Where They Buy

It is essential salespeople understand this headline. Market research long ago determined the top three reasons buyers buy what they do and where they do. The answers may surprise you.

The number one reason is they have the most trust and confidence in that business, product or people or all three. The key is to focus on trust and confidence building skills, which salespeople too frequently ignore so they can get to the close faster. Big mistake. This trust factor needs to be communicated in everything that touches a message to prospects. This is why brand names outsell off brands even if cheaper because the trust factor in them is higher. If buyers only bought the lowest price then Cricket would be the only phone, Costco the only store, and Kia the only car. And that is good news for you. Creating trust and confidence is something in your power. You can separate yourself from competitors by excelling at this. I have found that if I win this category, but am losing in the others, I may be given that crucial 'last look' at competitors' proposal to see if I can top it.

The fact trust is number one, and so important to customers' buying criteria, is great news for the small business because you can also beat the Internet at this one. Customers do not always have complete trust in a computer screen or a far away company. Will it get here on time? Can I try one out? Will I be able to speak to a real person? Can I get some local references? Will I know how to use it? Are they reliable? What if I am not happy with that model and need a different one? What if it doesn't look like the one pictured? Those are questions that go through buyers' minds that a local business answers much better.

Create trust the same way you do with another human being, be honest, responsive, listen, demonstrate competence, and show a track record. Make sure staff does the same. Display manners, stand behind your products and make them work. You can do that. All this has the simultaneous benefit to you and the customer of building the relationship and relationship selling is more important than ever.

Trying to inspire customer confidence is the reason companies advertise brand names or other braggadocio like "biggest" or "fastest growing" believing this message inspires trust. If your company and its reps are confident, it transfers to customers. If unconfident because you haven't mastered the product, understood customer needs, or, gotten behind in competence, this diminishes confidence. You can't give what you don't have so you will lose the sale, the money, and self-confidence. You and your company take a step backwards and may ruin otherwise good sales opportunities.

Do They Want It?

The number two reason buyers buy is they want it or need it. Plain and simple so sell products people want and need. General Motors sells cars we all need but continued to lose share until bankruptcy reorganization. It was because many did not want their cars so they bought someone else's. I have an exercise to prove to salespeople that want trumps price. I ask what they paid for their house. I then say, "I know there were homes there $25,000 less, why did you not buy one?" "It was not what we *wanted* comes the response. You can continue this exercise with other products, and I recommend you repeat all such exercises because salespeople must be shown three times before it stores.

People want good-looking things over not so much and *will pay extra for that*. They want bigger ones more than little ones and *will pay extra for it*, a faster one over a slower one, and *will pay more for that*. Want is a powerful motivator so work at making a customer want it and direct sales effort to getting them what they want. Our local movie theater has a self-service machine displaying colorful Willy Wonka hard candy of eight different kinds, each in a very tall clear tube. I wanted some! To get a load from one tube cost $1. The tube opened and candy slid down a long slide into your container. Loved watching this! I eventually swiped my credit card eight times for $8 just to watch the whole deal until my wife stopped me. I probably had $3 worth of candy and the owner a tidy profit. Again, people pay more for what they want. Your job is to make them want it.

Getting Your Price

Ranking third on the list of what makes people buy what they do is price. People usually buy the cheapest that *meets their needs*. Some, fewer of courses, pay the highest price to make a statement. Small businesses do not want constant price battles because selling on lowest price in the past has almost always been won by big box stores and the Internet. Selling on price is not even selling. We have eBay for that. You cannot succeed in small business being the low price leader. Be DIFFERENT enough from competitors so the decision does not come to price and so that you make margin. If always battling price that means you sell a commodity which means many others sell the same thing, which means time to sell other products.

There are two kinds of prices: those that support your business and those that customers accept. Hopefully they are close. If you sell on price you die on price not to mention price selling is no fun. Certainly deal some—say 15%—but keep a limit. Constantly battling price means customers do not see enough value so work on increasing it. Better than discounting is throwing in something the customer values at a retail price for which you pay wholesale. It is a big plus if the throw- in brings back service and/or supply revenue. Those "No Wait $19.99!" television commercials get this. They continue to throw in stuff until you cannot say no due to the perception of great value. I don't know if they make money but the deals set up a continuing relationship from which they hope to.

Buyers will pay more if they feel they get more and that is your work. Examples: we pay 25% more at a convenience store but don't care because we get convenience worth buying. We can pay the Post Office 45 cents to mail a letter but will pay FedEx ten dollars to do it quicker. We drive through Starbucks for high priced coffee in a hurry instead of cheap at home. Buyers everywhere assign additional value for additional ease so make sure you are providing it. Convenience and speed have emerged as the determining buying criteria for stressed Americans and it is important value added. Added value is what a business is supposed to bring to the customer experience. It is the salesperson's job to enunciate that and the owner's job to find good value to add. The value needs to be more than what is typically found in your market to win the deal. The French have a term for this called *lagniappe* meaning 'a little extra'.

You will hear one owner ask another "What is your value add?" A small business's value add is instruction about a product, enlightenment about a business problem, making something easier, doing something faster, repairing, doing something with higher quality, having friendlier staff and the like. To make a good living you do not want your value add to be lowest price but highest convenience! That means more profit and longevity. Convenience stores have been around a long time. expensive but, FedEx, expensive, but quick. Enterprise Car Rental is number one because they come to you. Expensive but is it really? Add stunning value, be different, charge a profitable price, and stay in business. Here are wise words on price selling versus value by John Buskin:

"It is unwise to pay too much but it is worse to pay too little. When you pay too much you lose a little money, that's all. When you pay too little you sometimes lose everything because the thing you bought was incapable of doing the thing you bought it to do. The common law of business balance prohibits paying a little and getting a lot-it can't be done. If you deal with the lowest bidder it is well to add something in for the risk you run. And if you do that you will have enough to pay for something better."

Amen.

Chocolate Bar Theory

When thinking about the price of your product keep in mind my Chocolate Bar Theory. Say you are in a store and come across a display of Godiva chocolate bars. They are considered the best chocolate and have a certain aura but they are, or are they, expensive? The Godiva bar costs five dollars and you can get a Hershey chocolate bar for one dollar that tastes pretty good too. You have a five-dollar bill in your pocket, think it within your range of pocket money, the Godiva bar is in front of you right now so you go for it and love it. Still, *you paid five times more than you had to!* You don't care because this amount of money is not consequential to your finances. You meant to buy chocolate but also wanted to buy the enjoyment of it all.

Buyers of anything can be like this. Sales reps, especially new ones, frequently make the mistake of fretting about the price of their product when the customer may not be. At least give them the opportunity to object to it before you do. Buyers frequently think the same way you did as you stared at the Godiva bar. They may want what you have, it is in their ballpark, you are there now and they like you. They may not feel like taking the time to shop around all creation because the time is not worth it to them. Just keep this in mind and don't talk yourself out of a decent sale nor drop your price needlessly.

Driver Of A Successful Salesperson

Belief in and passion for his products are top carries for a sales rep. He can't give what he doesn't have. If a salesperson is not sold on his product, full of enthusiasm and belief, excited about it, he can't inspire customers. They will not be enthusiastic either which costs sales. If the rep's product knowledge is weak the rep will not be respected as authoritative or perceived as an expert. The salesman must know! Give regular product knowledge tests to reps to ensure they keep up. Do not assume they are. Salespeople benefit greatly from sales training and it keeps them sharp. Plan monthly training sessions that practice role-playing, overcoming objections, pencil selling, prospecting tactics, crafting benefit statements and closing and demonstration skills. Of course rookies need a lot of this but veterans secretly like it too.

Continual training helps keep up passion for this craft that requires more of it than most jobs. Send new hires to a Dale Carnegie sales training program. It is worth the money. Sales training increases sales. Sales training pays for itself.

Here is the most effective sales lesson I ever got. I was a trainee and my hobby was golf. A trainer took me on a few calls and then we lunched. He probed for hobbies and asked questions about golf. "What is your farthest drive", he asked. "Oh man, I can tell you. It was nearly 300 yards at…." He asked what clubs I liked, what courses I played, why I liked the game. I answered with vigor and detail. Then he stopped me in mid sentence and explained why. "Did you notice how enthusiastically and knowledgeably you answered?" "No, not really." I was just talking about it and didn't think about that," I answered.

"Exactly the point," he said. "You were into it, credible and enthusiastic, and came across well. You were honest and convincing because of that. It was natural and from the heart and that is how you should sell. I don't golf but you made me want to. " Get there when selling and you will be a success. I did and…. I did. I have used this same training exercise for a long time with great effectiveness. Get a new rep talking about hobbies, children, whatever, but something they are knowledgeable and enthusiastic about and this important point will be understood. Once a salesperson is stocked with as much enthusiasm as product knowledge he can well become an invaluable high earning Revenue Ninja.

Stay Engaged!

Stay engaged. Stay engaged. Stay engaged. There, that should stress it. To make a sale, this discipline is your friend if you will just do it. Too often, we get a prospect, talk, come back a time or two, and the customer wants to think about it. The typical sales response is to do nothing for a period. Big mistake. Don't let your sales bandwidth go silent! No, you cannot keep going by and being a nuisance but can stay engaged by emailing interesting info on your product, then your company, on a customer testimonial, or on something totally different from what you are trying to sell. Send a link to a pertinent video. It is doubtful any of these annoy the customer but they sure keep you in a good light while he thinks or looks at other vendors. If silent during his 'thinking time' then he is silent about you.

When selling something people expect you to put forth a sales effort. You want to be persistent, yes, professionally persistent, which is doing it without irritating the customer. Doing this lets the prospect know what kind of contact and service to expect after the sale. Too many sales are hit and run. Customers want to experience that trust and confidence feeling, which is your goal while working this semi-slow, stay engaged period. Keep generic articles, product info and testimonials ready for an email. It takes persistence to succeed in sales and staying engaged is part of that. Staying engaged means keeping up a regular presence after the sale. The main reason is *customers continue to buy!* Keep yourself positioned for more sales with regular engagement by letting them know of your other offerings.

The Wagon Is Full

We have talked exclusively about the sales expertise your company carries or not. The same importance goes for product inventory. It is much easier to acquire than selling expertise since you just buy it but you do need means to do so. To be successful selling Wonder Widgets have them in stock. You can't sell what you don't have, what buyers cannot see, touch and try. You cannot sell out of an empty wagon. To specialize into Wonder Widgets models 13 b and 16c, stock them to be seen and sold. This demonstrates you have the product expertise customers expect as well. Taking the shortcut saying "I don't have it but I can get it " means you try to sell things you do not have which does not work well. Upstarts frequently try to shoestring inventory and it is not a good idea. Low inventory means low sales and higher inventory usually means more sales. Product inventory, the right inventory, is a vitally important business logistic. It only takes a check, good judgment and purchase order. When people buy anything today they want it today.

Sales Rep Sharing

There should be no disagreement that the best way to grow business is employing salespeople capable of good sales calls and a number of them. They have also read this book and are fluent in the sales techniques. The trouble is good sales reps are expensive. Give a trainee $2500 a month salary plus commission and an accomplished rep in your industry double that. The wise owner looks at a good rep as "free" because real ones bring in more than they cost. There are ways to ease hiring if cash flow can't handle it. One is to provide a 90 day guarantee and then go to straight commission. You have no risk but likely not have this employee long either because most reps want a decent salary.

Another is sales sharing similar to time sharing. Split a rep with another company each sharing the pay. This rep sells the two different product lines to the same customers. If the buyers are not interested in product A they may be in product B. This is good for the rep providing more commission opportunities than from just one company. Go further, if need be, and split three ways. You don't want to keep it this way but it can get you ramped up with the least pain. Once you have one who supports himself hire on another and repeat. This is how you grow.

Another pay plan I like is the *non-recovered draw*. Reps always want something to count on and owners want the rep to be profitable thus the two can be hard to reconcile leading to tension. The unrecoverable draw method meets this problem in the middle. Say you have a $2500 salary plus $1000 recoverable draw against commission. If the rep has a few bad months the draw owed back to the company may get onerous and de-motivating. To prevent that you let the draw for the month be non-recoverable if not met and it does not carry forward. However, if the next month the rep makes above draw that month's draw only is subtracted from that month's commissions. It is a way of splitting the risk.

Dealing With Sales Menopause

I hate to end on this note but it is a sales reality that salespeople fade in their mid forties—a sort of sales menopause. It is going to happen and you may need to make adjustments for it. Energy begins to drop as does the self start and nuclear work ethic. They begin to judge, by looking at the outside of a building, if someone is a prospect. Each prospect is clutched ever tighter as fewer are in the pipeline. Life goals are different. Physical and mental fitness begin to decline. You no longer like to prospect. More stress management is needed to stay even. The senior rep may engage more frequently in 'internal selling' which is trying to sell the boss on special concessions he can offer customers to make the selling easier.

One reason for fade, and this happens to owners, is lost passion, the magic ju ju that overcomes objections and obstacles to making a sale. Seasoned reps get mind ninja-ed from all the lost sales that piled up even among the many made. This does not have to end anyone's career but it is wise to move to management or training work in the mid-forties. Look ahead to hiring a rookie to break in and re-energize the place with his charming personality, good looks, good dress, good humor and enthusiasm! Give them an arithmetic test that shows they can figure percentages, work with decimal points and compute gross profit. Hire someone around 30 with high energy, competitiveness, lean build, good communication skills, a sense of urgency and discipline. The best salespeople are ones you train.

There is turnover in sales work, more than any other. It is just the nature of it. It is a self cleaning profession similar to professional athletes because of the higher intensity demands of their job. For this reason have salespeople sign a non-compete agreement. Sales reps learn your pricing, your strategies and your account base so that is reason enough. You do not want them walking to competitors and turning around taking your customers. The law protects you and it will save you from losing customers and profits. You normally get protection from the rep calling on your customers, the ones he gained knowledge of working for you, but generally not from calling on new ones. Some states allow barring reps from completely working in the same field. The legal basis for all this centers around laws protecting 'trade secrets' which is intellectual property, developed by any company, at its expense, including customer lists. Non-compete contracts are typically for one to three years. To be enforceable, some money, say $100 a month, has to be paid to the rep in return for signing the agreement. That is how any contract works and makes it much easier to enforce.

Good job getting to this point in the chapter! Writing about sales technique can get a little starchy. But learning the ways and means of effective salesmanship can be stimulating. Books on sales technique sell like crazy. I think all that there is to master shows we can answer the sometimes heard question as to whether salespeople are born or made. They are made. For some of the best material on this topic read anything by Tom Hopkins, Og Mandino and Jeffery Gitomer. These are among the top selling sales book authors of all time and know the sales profession. The best-selling business book of all is mainly about selling and written by Dale Carnegie. *How To Win Friends and Influence People* is still in print after 15 million copies. Each of these authors has a different style for sure. Gitomer's book bindings are way cool.

Networking Groups

This is a get together of owners and salespeople who meet to obtain sales leads from peers. Their organizers put up a web page listing members and what they do, which is usually free, and for good reason. These membership pages do not provide much value other than saying who is a member. Yay for us! I watched such a group grow to 700 members. You could blog and say what you wanted. Regular events were held and all the rest. There was a lot of glad handing, big smiles, and for a bit everyone felt important while egos received massaging. That was the high point. It struck me as mostly vanity and after a couple years it folded because the value was not there.

It would be a mistake to attend networking groups thinking buyers for your product are there. It can happen but most are sellers with precious few buyers so go to make fruitful connections. Some networkers think this is how you obtain all your business and routinely schlep from group to group. Big mistake. You may be hoping to bypass the heavier lifting, but more fruitful effort, of prospecting on actual customers. Prospecting on customers *is* networking. It's better than that because you reach real buyers directly. If you are going to network do it with customers! Hold open houses or lunch and learns to secure prospects. If selling is not your cup of tea, then get the means to hire a real salesperson that likes it. Doing too much networking and not much prospecting means you need a course correction.

Networking groups like to hold functions, maybe for a fee. Sometimes an All Knowing Speaker is brought in. Again, this does not lead to much business and is probably more group therapy. Certain leaders may speak which may or may not be helpful. There is one networking group that is outstanding and worth the money for a year or two, which is BNI. Their model means business and this group is nationwide. BNI charges $300 to join and only one from any industry is allowed. BNI holds members accountable for submitting leads and if you miss a meeting without getting a sub you are kicked out. A chapter, which is comprised of around 20 members, makes sure each member understands the type of customer other members are seeking. As they go about prospecting, they are, in a sense, also prospecting for the other members and vice versa. In this sense, you have 19 salespeople. I have routinely spent the money and sent reps to belong to a chapter.

Marketing

"Never stop marketing". This was the response from a fellow business owner when I asked what she thought was the most important thing to do to stay in business. Marketing is not my strong suit but I can speak to it as a non-expert, which is where you may be. I am meat and potatoes on marketing and use basic proven stuff. Making sales calls, canvassing and working a sales territory is a marketing method as good as any. "Feet on the street" is number one on my marketing methods because I have control and it brings actual human reconnaissance. It is the original social media. It is going to be difficult for any small business to match the marketing presence of a bigger company but by making a sales call, with a well-heeled rep, puts you on a pretty even keel with any other human presence. So a good sales call can be a great equalizer.

Sales and marketing go hand in hand. Good marketing produces warm leads for salespeople. It needs to make the phone ring. Forget about spending money trying to create an image or paint a business Picasso. Full marketing efforts directed by an advertising agency are usually out of the financial reach of a small business. What is useful to small business is guerrilla marketing which means unconventional or atypical. It could be stunt marketing, cash mobs, trade shows, Groupon coupons, lunch and learns, or public relations events. Guerrilla marketing relies on creative thought, effort, and time spent executing rather than spending on media. The father of guerrilla marketing, Jay Conrad Levinson, tells this humorous story to illustrate the mind of the guerrilla marketer.

> *There were three competitors on a street right next to each other. The one in the middle was the smallest of the three and the two on each end were large, well-funded businesses. The two large competitors had a huge sale going at the same time and were on radio and TV. One put up a banner nearly covering the entire store that said "50%*

Off Everything." The other large business did similar with an even larger banner that read: " Will Beat All Competitors Offers". The small guy in the middle, seeing all this, had a banner made up for his store too that read: "Main Entrance."

Marketing can mean anything from pens to billboards. Every business should have, as a minimum, an up to date web site, e-mail marketing, social media presence—especially multiple You Tube videos—company brochure, downloadable product information, invoice stuffers, telemarketing, and running a small ad on a regular basis in a good publication to build name recognition. I know a woman's dress shop that has grown 30% during the recession by putting up pictures of its fashions *everyday* on Facebook. I know a green house/ nursery growing using just Craigslist and Facebook. For best effect of social media, or any advertising really, it must be regular and repetitive. Get all you can from social media if only for the simple reason it is free. But keep in mind that it is called social media and not business media for a reason. You cannot conduct any commerce on social media like you can on a website. There are no shopping carts.

An effective marketing method of medium expense, is a direct mail campaign using post cards. Do one campaign each quarter. Utilize 5x6 cards, or larger, and abide by Marketing 101 meaning they make an offer. Post cards have gained favor because there is nothing to open, they have the lowest postage and the receiver can quickly view both sides without much effort. If you follow up a direct mail campaign with a phone call to each recipient you increase favorable responses.

A good response from is 1%, yes 1%, so if you mail 1,000 pieces ten qualified responses is a good response (you might use that as a yardstick to measure the effectiveness of other marketing methods). Cost for the purchase and mailing of these postcards is $2500 for 1500 pieces. To buy a telemarketing list with names and phone numbers may be $225 for a 1,000 names. Direct mail and telemarketing lists have gotten quite specialized. For example, you can buy just beauticians, morticians, electricians, CFO,s, landscaping business owners etc. The purchase of these lists is money well spent to get business plus it is an action to stimulate sales activity if it is lagging. Try Sales Genie or Info USA.

I like taking the same list and having a telemarketer call it to set appointments for salespeople. The lists have gotten so good you can really pinpoint the contact you want. I give a telemarketer a base salary and then $75 for each valid appointment. If it turns into a sale the telemarketer gets $200 more for that. A good telemarketer will more than pay for himself.

I have another piece of unscientific marketing information on what people read. I know this from writing a business column for two years for a paper that tracked readership. The most read columns contain numerical rankings. It seems people cannot resist reading headlines like "The Ten Most Important Business Trends of the Century." Or "The Top Ten Plays Of The Year" Or "The Ten Best Cupcake Recipes of All Time." David Letterman's show, for the past 15 years, features their Top Ten lists. You just cannot resist reading the whole list to find out who is number one. Whatever. People cannot resist reading rankings.

Keep things short. That is the first commandment in the marketing world for all messages. Some notable ones: "Got Milk?". "Just Do It." "Absolutely Positively Overnight." "I've Got Your Back" (a chiropractor). "It's Not Delivery It's Digorno." Five words would be considered long. Company names are likewise brief and best be one word. Sometimes even that is felt to be too long so companies go to three letters, think IBM, UPS, AT&T, even though they stand for something longer. It may be that we will reduce our alphabet by ten letters one day to make everyone be even briefer. We have the attention span of a mayfly with Alzheimer's and don't remember much.

You can get top notch advice from a marketing pro if on a budget, which you are, and here is how. Marketing companies want to sell services which is fine if you can use them. But you are not going to be in the market for most of them. Make an appointment with a marketing expert and offer to pay for this time, say $200 an hour. Ask away and hand him a check when the hour is up and you should have your money's worth. Have you ever seen an expert in anything not eager to talk about it much less get paid to do so?

Should you engage an ad agency be diligent to keep the mission on how they are going to help you sell more stuff. Agency speak can get windy from discussing demographics, market segmentation, impressions per minute, eyeballs, market penetration, circulation, ratings and all the rest. Tell them you really don't know much about that, you are glad they do, but ask what their estimate is of much more stuff this will sell and that is the only metric you are interested in.

I close the sales chapter with the most popular column I ever wrote. It circulated the Internet and is a metaphor for the ideal behavior towards customers and how to get their business. I hope you enjoy it. Bow wow.

A Dog Is Entrepreneur's Best Mentor
By Tom Pease

Is it possible most things we need to learn about business we can learn from a dog? They can be brilliant business instructors. Their No. 1 lesson: loyalty. Is there anything more loyal than your dog? He greets so enthusiastically whether you deserve it or not. Can you imagine the extra business duplicating that with customers? We love that our loyal dog is always available. It waits for us to call upon it-always there ready to respond to any interest shown it. Do we take the same stance towards customers? Dogs teach us to minimize our words and get to the point. Dogs can talk but only know one word. All dog communication is accomplished with this one sound. Boy, you humans waste a lot of time talking. Bow wow!

When totally exhausted we are 'dog tired'. This is because a dog gives everything until it can't. If we work every day until dog tired then we will be successful. Dogs are as sincere as Mother Teresa talking to the sick. You cannot fail to respond to its suggestions when looking into those undistracted, totally focused eyes. It gets them what they want. Take a lesson all salespeople. And speaking of salespeople could they learn to be better prospectors watching the determined digging done by dogs? There is no better example of 'being in the moment' than a dog. It gives undivided attention and is focused on you, what you are doing and saying right now. Can we do that with customers and employees? We need to.

Dogs teach things above and beyond human comprehension. They are always excited to see you even if you are boring. They forget about any previous inattention if you will make it right, right now! They are focused on the relationship come what may. Can you say that? A dog is brave. No matter their size it will protect its owner. Even 10 pound yapper dogs bark at you with everything they have if they think you are threatening its owner. Owners want employees guarding their business similarly.

Dogs have worked their way into the vernacular used to judge performance, superior or not so. If you are the winner you are Top Dog. If you are not so then you are the Underdog. If neither the winner or loser but at least flashy you are a Hot Dog. Disappointment is expressed saying "dog-gone-it!" So in high competition arenas of business and sports the dog is the standard. We can only hope our employees accept specialized training as well as dogs and match their superhuman accomplishments. They are trained to sniff out cancer, track down criminals, become seeing eyes, and perform search and rescue (could one be trained to sell?). Surely, then, we can learn that new technology, software or sales training so we accomplish our business missions. Next time you seek business advice take a walk in your dog's tracks instead.

So it is true, nothing happens until somebody sells something. Now that you have the how-to on all that let's look at the next chapter on the best things to be selling.

Moe's summation: "Dogs understand salesmanship. We are masters. We get what we want using few sounds but excel using non-verbal selling skills. When in sales mode our face appears as sincere as a chocolate chip cookie. Our ears are up. Our attention is undivided. Our eyes are solely focused on our victim. We may tilt our head. We wag our tail with enthusiasm. All this body language will close the deal."

4

Characteristics Of
The Best Businesses
To Be In

W hat are the best businesses to be in? That is a question any business person should regularly ask no matter if starting out, re-evaluating the present business or thinking about diversifying. Some are absolutely better than others and choosing wrongly could prove fatal. Cue music from *Mission Impossible* and its famous: "Your mission, should you choose to accept it......" Choosing right, on the other hand, is rewarding. We know you can't choose the weather or parents but you do choose your business. Let this chapter guide in finding a mission that is a lasting.

Look at products you buy regularly—cell minutes, insurance, soap, food, utilities, cleaning services, repair services, cosmetics, lawn maintenance, sanitizer, bug killers, supplies, education, alarm monitoring, tuition, food, medical, electronics, diabetes supplies, batteries, toner, music and delivery. Pay particular attention to those under contract like insurance, HVAC maintenance, cable subscriptions, magazines, newspapers, pest control, Internet connection, your NFL package, alarm monitoring, rent, and email. You consider these recurring necessities—part of everyday living. These are the most durable segments to build a lasting business—those that are necessities and have a recurring need.

Entrepreneur magazine lists quick-serve businesses, senior care businesses, and cleaning specialties as the top three successful franchises. Look about your city and note long-standing businesses and those with cars in the parking lot. There are longevity clues there. For other insight, scan the Yellow Pages, which, yes, are still being printed. You find full page color ads, really expensive, for businesses like plumbers, landscapers, HVAC dealers and attorneys. This tells you there is money, profitable money, there. Take note of the small ads, too.

Would you want to own a business aligned with those or put money on untried technology or invention? Do you want long-term success or short-term excitement? That is the dilemma you face as a business owner. It is not a hard decision if your goal is to make a living running your own enterprise. Most long lasting businesses are not based on new moon shot technology but a reinvention of well-established necessity business segments that you give new twists.

Other long lasting businesses, even lasting longer than a lifetime, accomplish this servicing their adversary, but also recurring patron, *the forces of nature*. This characteristic is broad. These are things that grow, move, threaten, things needed for health, life, education, cleanliness, human happiness, and things needed to keep other things working. These are great business categories because they never go away. Humans also create forces of necessity like sports, technology, entertainment, vanity, competition, energy consumption, conservation, and automobiles.

Recurring necessities are found in abundance servicing things like vehicles, humans, machines and nature. These areas may be landscapes, software, waistlines, fitness, safety, food, insurance, fingernails, education, potholes, dogs, dust, buildings, and making money. Mold, grass, computer networks, crops, trees, insects and burglaries are growing and necessitate services that contain those. The guideline words are must and necessity. You must eat, sleep, age, clean, play, work, transport, stay safe, plug it in, insure it, communicate, put tires on it, heat it, cool it, protect it and get stuff fixed because stuff is always wearing.

All these categories are found in households and businesses alike. There are way more consumers than businesses but any one business buys considerably more stuff than any one consumer.

"Create repeat business by building it in."

The second most important business longevity characteristic is that the business sells products that 'eat and drink'. Eaters and drinkers are hardware products that, once placed, generate additional revenue streams of required service, supply or support. A computer system is an example requiring all three. When you sell hardware that requires servicing and supplying you make three sales for the price of one. Not only that, but their recurring revenue streams of service, supply and support continue for years and surpass the hardware sale. The most famous eater-drinker is the razor which commits a lifetime of purchasing blades and cream which is an amount far greater than razors. It is a recurring necessity to shave because nothing keeps hair or whiskers from growing. There is a model for you.

Selling eaters and drinkers keeps you out of the commodity zone. Selling only hardware makes you vulnerable to the Internet. If you do not have any eaters and drinkers why are you not adding a few? Why sell just hardware when you should be making three sales for the price of one?

Iconic examples are Apple "i" products. Apple stuff is a monstrous eater and drinker *and* a force of nature under human happiness. It's slick hardware but that's not what made Apple America's most valued company. It is because they originate some 12 revenue streams like air time, video, movies, books, apps, songs, email, voice mail, advertising, batteries, repair, accessories, and texting—a lot of lucrative eating and drinking. Apple has the most consummate after-market revenue producing products ever. One hardware sale automatically makes 12 more sales along with it! You won't have a 12-tentacle revenue sucking eater and drinker like this but just getting one with two or three is good. How many tentacles does your business have?

Heavy Drinkers

There are similar heavy drinkers like ink jet and laser printers. HP practically gives you the printer to sell high profit ink cartridge—real thirst quenchers! On their heels comes Cartridge World, which refills cartridges, a business servicing a recurring necessity. 3D printers are getting very hot. Cinemas know a movie ticket literally means eating and drinking revenue from very high margin drinks, popcorn and candy. Selling a Harley brings repair, chrome accessories, endless clothing and logo merchandise. Diabetic testing supplies live in this category. Car dealers sell the car, then financing, extended warranties, insurance and, of course, parts, labor and accessories or body work. A new comer provides batteries for mobile devices: Batteries Plus. Mobility is a new recurring necessity requiring batteries, many batteries.

Upstart SodaStream is intent on letting you make carbonated drinks replacing the usual brand names in cans and bottles. SodaStream sells a $130 device that turns regular water into carbonated water using CO_2 cartridges and flavored syrup which you buy with regularity. SodaStream is doing well at $500 million revenue and, surprise (not) say their profits come from the cartridges and flavor packs. Heavy drinking going well here. Gobie Co.is selling individual water bottles that have a filter in them for the purest water. Of course, you need to change it regularly.

You replace HVAC filters regularly, your oil, get a car wash, and buy many diapers for the tyke. How about treadmill service? On the Inc. 500 fastest growing is Treadmilldoctor.com. Of course. We are a fat country that continuously battles bulges by wielding treadmills that break under all that weight. So Treadmill Doctor sells repair parts nationwide, treadmills, and of course, treadmill work out clothing! Eating … drinking. Eating … drinking. Here is one I have only seen once but it fits: Dryer Vent Man. Yes, clothes always throw lint so Dryer Vent Man keeps the exhaust clean and utility bill lower. Dryer Vent Man also installs a re-route to re-circulate warm dryer air into the house saving energy so he serves two recurring necessities. How about Mobile Home Laser Leveler? Time and gravity will always push many things out of whack so this business puts them back straight.

My business, copiers, eats and drinks streams of paper, toner, and maintenance to keep it fed. I do not make the machine but sell one to create the recurring revenue streams. If you can sell the machine that sets up the eating and drinking you control your destiny better. If not, just servicing recurring demand set in motion otherwise is a promising business model like hair dressers, plumbers, electrical companies, weight loss, senior services, restaurants, women's nails, tire dealers, fitness centers, restaurants, vehicle repair, computer networks, and health care.

Heating and air conditioning companies service the recurring necessity that humans must be warmed and cooled. We live six days without water, one without smelling, so plumbers are safe and providers of liquids in all forms, including ice making, are here forever. Restaurateurs know we have to eat very regularly and feed us. They have to be supplied so farmers feed them and grocery stores too. You recall the California Gold Rush of 1849. Not many prospectors struck it rich but those supplying the food, drink and supplies to them did. If you were a businessperson it was better to be a supplier than a gold digger. The same goes for today.

Realtors sell homes because humans must have shelter, especially the 3 million new Americans born yearly. When outside we require clothing for weather, recreation, sports or employment so clothiers feed that. Security companies install burglar or fire alarms meeting steady need for safety and, most importantly, there is a monthly fee for monitoring. Delivery companies cater recurring demands that we want it now and bring it to me. These necessities are driven by human nature or nature's nature which ensures continual need like a Memphis landscape company's sign 'Since 1938'.

Messy Mother Nature creates numerous repetitive cleaning businesses whether the Statue of Liberty, 50 story office buildings, teeth, carpet, swimming pools, painting, oil changing or rust prevention. We can learn something about built in repeat business from Hallmark card shops. They have a card for any month, even day, of the year. There are the holidays like Valentines, Christmas and Thanksgiving that recur and produce card sales. If no holiday there are always sick people so get well cards are needed as are friendship cards, weddings, sympathy cards and on and on for built in repeat demand.

You get the idea—sell products requiring service, supplies or support, on a regular basis, that are necessities. This is where lasting businesses live. Contrast this with businesses selling one-and-done products that, once sold, end any relationship because they create no recurring demand. If selling, say, mailboxes, microwave ovens, exercise equipment, carpeting, lamps, pillows, birdfeeders, dresses or lawn furniture, there is no aftermarket revenue nor are they necessities. Most retail stores sell these. They sell products we like but there is no built in necessity demand to return thus they have the highest failures. Maybe better to be a shoe cobbler.

A Memphis dry cleaning chain recently celebrated 100 years in business. These industries, and those like them, will always be necessities, reoccur, and can't be outsourced overseas. Professionals like doctors, lawyers, engineers, architects, and scientists meet critical recurring necessities and can become long-term businesses too. Frequently though, they are so good at what they do that they are so bad as business owners. The professional who can move out of his profession, become entrepreneurial and form a group of fellow professionals can build a sizable business. There are plenty of them.

Businesses in my examples can scale large or sell franchises. Hair cutting has Sport Clips and Fantastic Sam's on a national level. Weight loss has Jenny Craig. Muffler repair has Midas Muffler. Plumbers have Roto-Rooter. Some successful real estate agents formed Century 21 and ReMax, both national. There is Orkin in pest control. All started small and meet recurring necessities. Millionaires are minted among these recurring necessity providers from their eating and drinking servicing skills.

I share writings with my brother Mike, ex-Navy diver, who has a boat maintenance business. He fights ongoing battles with salt-water assaults on boat hulls. He tangles with barnacles, sea squirts and corrosion — stuff always needing battling. We reviewed this chapter and he summed it up: "You are saying make sure you get repeat business." Yes.

An Element of The Mundane

Most of these industries have another surprising commonality: an element of the mundane. There is nothing glamorous about cutting grass, hair, cleaning, pet grooming, fixing HVAC, installing or monitoring alarm systems, wiring, changing filters, chasing computer viruses, rust prevention, teeth cleaning, making cement, farming, educating, repairing machines, setting up machines, selling insurance, fighting barnacles, providing water flow, selling windows, making ice or killing bugs. That would true of large companies, too, like UPS/FedEx who just deliver. There is nothing glamorous about delivery. Delivery guys get hot, sweat, produce dirty laundry and burn carbon. Yet these delivery companies are worldwide meeting the recurring demand of delivery, here since the invention of the wheel. They stay in business.

Businesses dealing in the mundane—but certainly utilizing best practices—are easily distinguished from those seeking the cutting edge by the larger amounts of money they make and their greater time in business. I think of Two Men and a Truck that has scaled national as an example. 1-800-Got Junk has done similar. Heck, somebody might go nationwide with 1-800-Chainsaw. If you operate, say, a fish hatchery, rock quarry, run a logging or railroad tie business, you face little threat from smart phones, the Internet or commodity bazooka. Similarly profitable areas with longevity not likely to be made obsolete by the Internet or commoditized are:

- Marketing firms
- Senior Services
- Construction companies
- Animal husbandry
- Medical testing
- Temporary staffing

- Wedding planner
- Vehicle care
- Internet services
- Security/fire
- Repair
- Freight/transportation
- Sales
- Instruction/education
- Pest control
- Recycling
- Refrigeration
- Funeral/burial
- Food/agriculture
- Child care
- Sports
- Engineering
- Women's cosmetics
- Hospice
- Green energy
- Rehab

Entrepreneurs fall victim to "exciting" products that do not make a good business such as Incredible Edibles. They make gorgeous mouth watering edible table pieces formed like flowers or character cookies and are certainly exciting. Yet, the labor is intensive and since it is a food, has to be baked, colored, and has freshness expiration dates plus regulations making it hard to inventory and scale. People want these yet the owners have a hard time all the same with these limitations. The lesson is ensure that it is your *business* that is exciting above even what it sells or does.

The Problem With Tech Business

The higher up the technology chain the more glamorous and less mundane it might be. Using cloud-based computing, an ISP and a cell phone one can produce some kind of tech start up for $1,000 but so can thousands of other competitors. These business models are threatened with obsolescence from technology, *and soon*, by power players with dollars to innovate but even they get horribly sick. Most of those businesses come with an expiration date. There is a graveyard of examples. Yahoo is not well. Best Buy, the biggest electronics retailer, is nearly unprofitable and firing 2400. HP cut 29,000. Blackberry maker Research In Motion fired 30% of its workforce. At this writing Sharp Electronics was laying off 10,000 worldwide and looking for a buyer. Most copier manufacturers have merged. Panasonic laid off 39,000 people in 2011. Even Apple's iTunes juggernaut is now declining and threatened from subscription services like Spotify and Pandora which changed even the great seer Steve Job's premise that people want to own their music.

Long term high-tech successes are few for small businesses and, as you can see, tough for big ones too. Sectors associated with tech get buried and blind-sided. Look at how smart phones eliminated checks, maps, watches, wallets, cash, cameras, radios, alarms, printed matter, music stores, bookstores, land lines, GPS sales, laptop sales, and advertising mediums. This represents a lot of damage to tech related businesses (tech eating tech) and again, this is just not a safe arena for a small business. Entire tech segments are vulnerable to just new code writing from a talented programmer! Stay clear! Don't go there.

And I am not saying your business be a world of mundane, certainly use the newest tech to run it, but your product needs this base element to reduce volatility. Should you make a sound, exciting business from the mundane and it last, and it meet your needs, provide freedom and provide fulfillment, *it will be thrilling*! Going out of business is not.

What is exciting, and should be the reasons to own a business in the first place, is enjoying customer relationships, making sales, hiring great people, a team pulling hard together, promoting your workers, obtaining profitability, enjoying your freedom, forming vendor relationships, building business value, making your living, and moving into retirement with it! I never tire of that. There are numerous business segments, ones that will live long and help its owner do the same, if the entrepreneur brings the expertise and business ability. No point having a business that won't take you far, that gets airborne only to fall from the sky. *Small Business Survival 101* suggests these lasting directions, not living for flash bulb moments or fleeting headlines and then you are gone. There is a lot of that.

Internet Proofing

The mundane element may seem to clash with sound business advice that says make yourself new and exciting to differentiate from competition. Mundane implies 'me too' which seems not to win the day. This is absolutely a good point. This paradox is answered by our Federal Express example. Again, all they do is deliver—a service around since the Stone Age and amongst plenty of competition. The Internet is no threat to their business. FedEx ADDS VALUE, exciting value, to a mundane industry like overnight speed, same day, international, and real time tracking, to delivery and became a global phenomenon. I am sure it is scintillating to be Fred Smith and I doubt he complains his company just delivers. Another example of adding value to the mundane is a 100 year old Christie Cut Stone. They target large rocks stuck in Mother Earth, extract them and transport them to their shop. There a computer controlled machine cuts and shapes the stone into all sizes which is then used in construction. No computer, software, or Internet will ever threaten this business.

Protect your future from the Internet by adding irreplaceable value to your business by combining a mundane element with a high service one. You can do so and become the greatest thing in your city, recognized even as the latest thing, by adding things like speed, convenience, competence, location, selection, and appeal, to name a few, to any business not known for them. For example, Netflix became a huge convenience success just by mailing movies to your mailbox. Nothing new about movies or mailboxes. A real estate chain has sold Wal Mart on letting it set up in its stores to sell homes and benefit from the foot traffic. There is nothing new about Wal Mart and realtors.

Both these business models were redone to add value to them for the customer and everyone is a winner.

The mundane element helps keep the Internet and automation away. Most of these categories will not be automated out of business. There are not many machines that can replace a human in these more mundane categories whereas those in 'high tech' segments would be most vulnerable. Combine the mundane with a knowledge-based service for a good combo. FedEx does mundane delivery but combines it with knowledge to get packages through customs or across the ocean. A machine cannot come to your home or business or get you through customs. Automation and software do threaten even knowledge businesses so stay ahead of that or sell automation. Monitor Apps to see the future. Maybe take your knowledge, hire a developer, and sell your own app. This way you too can be a Master of The Universe until somebody updates that.

Don't sell easily recognizable name brands to protect yourself from losing sales to the Internet, especially if you have a store. Retailers are vulnerable today to a practice called *show rooming*. Show rooming is when prospective buyers come to your facility to see and try a product but then go home to buy it off the Internet. Will retailers need to institute 'cover charges' at their stores to compensate for show rooming? It is much harder to show room your product if your brand is not so known or if your product requires additional value added expertise from a dealer before it is useable.

Create The Demand

The ideal product to sell is one that creates repeat business by actually building that into the product. I have given the example of products similar to a copier that, once placed, immediately create new demand streams of service, supply or support. You can create demand and repeat demand another way and here is how. My daughter gave me six woodworking lessons from a local shop. I went and got hooked. I bought a table saw for $2,000 which then required more stuff to work wood.

I returned to buy wood, glue, finishes, sealers, books, plans, fasteners, blades, more classes and widgets.

My wife likes sewing so I bought her quilting lessons. That was years ago. She bought a quilting machine for $3000 which required presses, irons, patterns, needles, weird looking guide things, cutters, jelly rolls and something called a fat quarter. She continuously has a quilt in the making, buying cloth, thread, design patterns, magazines and do dads. She joined a guild, pays dues and goes to meetings. She still takes lessons at the Quilting Barn. They created a monster and stimulated the global economy! So create demand by advertising, offering seminars, paid lessons, lunch and learns on what you sell, then service the recurring demand that comes with it.

I took on a new product, a commercial water purifier that replaces water jug systems. Jugs are un-green and labor intensive but unchanged since 1950 speaking to the power of our principle. Water coolers service the recurring necessity that humans must have water to live. It can't be replaced thus water jug companies have been since Egyptians balanced them on their heads. Enter the filtering unit that does not require jugs but does require filter replacement and a bit of maintenance. Filter changing is a built in demand to keep water pure. Customers also buy a lifetime of paper cups! This meets my example of a mundane product that eats and drinks.

Internet vs. You

What should we make of the Internet's threat to your business? Not nearly what you frequently hear. Like we just saw, the mundane is unfazed by it but does utilize it. Look around your city. Streets are still busy while drivers patronize businesses, which, at least on main thoroughfares, are plentiful. Malls have lots of cars and strip centers are mostly full, at least on weekends. There is a huge Bass Pro Shop opening in Memphis. A new Walgreens goes up on some corner seemingly weekly. I still get a newspaper in my driveway, magazines in my mailbox and can go to a bookstore and buy a book. Car dealerships still stock cars as far as your eye can focus.

Sporting goods, jewelry stores, clothing stores, motorcycle shops, hardware stores, are all staying in business which shows the Internet bark is louder than its bite since these type businesses are most vulnerable to it. You sometimes hear stores are not needed, you can't compete with online shopping, don't need a salesperson, and blah, blah, blah. Both online and offline scenarios have proved viable and coexist. Both prosper because there are ever more customers being born.

Even with advertising dollars going to the Internet this has not been enough to knock out traditional mediums although it has made some smaller. There are still billboards, Yellow Pages, mailers, magazine and newspaper advertising. Radio and TV stations in our city are not closing because of the Internet. There seems to be enough to go around for coexistence. This past Sunday the paper was jammed full of advertising circulars, flyers and advertising booklets that took me a while to throw out so I could get to the paper. Those things cost a fortune so they must still be working.

There has certainly been Internet Mania the past ten years predicting the doom of just about everything but it has not happened. I think the wise consumer and business owner give it its due but do not make the mistake of going all in on it.

Consider that in 2000 the population was 282,000,000. Today it is 312,000,000. That is 40 million more customers needing recurring services. In 1990, the census revealed a population of 248 million, people so that is 60 million new customers for the economy since then. A growing population is an economic growth engine and rising tide that lifts all boats.

The Internet lessons are that a majority prefer to kick tires, look at the merchandise, try it out, try it on, take the spouse along, ask for help, and enjoy "going shopping." Turning on a computer does not do it for them. Those that want that can enjoy that process so on-liners and off-liners are served. Most Internet-vulnerable businesses have added Internet sales departments that help their business by serving both segments.

My wife shops both. She says if you know what you want the Internet will do but you wait days to get it which is no competition for the instant gratification she gets hauling stuff home. She prefers seeing things in three dimension that physical shopping provides vs. one-dimensional online shopping. It's good to remember shoppers always shopped around before buying. The Internet, here 25 years, did not change that or enable that it just made the buying process quicker than walking the Yellow Pages or getting three bids. "Let Your Fingers Do the Walking" was the first form of Internet shopping.

For the small business owner it is prudent to continue in knowledge-based businesses that sell hardware requiring service, support, supplies and salespeople rather than selling self-explanatory hardware only. It is pretty hard to Google up much competition with a business that knows the ins and outs of proprietary software or designing custom made goods or filing electronic medical record rebates for doctors.

It is even better for a small business owner to be in a business in which customers demand a high confidence. The Internet is trustworthy but has opportunities for cyber theft. You don't know the people on the other end or where they are. A business with a physical location and known people will enjoy a higher level of trust.

The Internet is good at selling hardware but poor at the supporting services small businesses are good at. The Internet does not come to you: you go to it. Even people on the other end, although they may be in your city, are more likely out of state and can't come to you. Small businesses have the personal response and personal service issue advantage over the Internet. Should this technology encroach on you then slowly move to a related industry that requires a value add. Those will always be with us too.

Inbound Or Outbound Effort

Once clear on the recurring demand to support decide on an inbound or outbound effort. Or both? Inbound means a retail facility where customers come to you. Outbound means you go to them. I much prefer the latter. Retail locations are high failure and rely on location plus expensive real estate, and give up a lot in owner control. Regular advertising is a necessity. These businesses are good and then not, and in my opinion, come with an expiration date. All it takes to hurt you is a competitor opening nearby or the area to decline—neither in your control. If going retail shore it up with outbound sales efforts. You have control of outbound efforts and failure statistics are lower. There is nothing keeping you from making 25 calls a day hunting business or 50.

It is up to you and your level of determination. You can be as determined as you want in inbound, polishing your store and all, but that may have little to do with customer's patronizing you. Most good business deals I accomplish come from outbound marketing efforts, going to see a man about a horse. If you want to see the horse, the business opportunity, its size means you go to it. The horse is not coming to you and neither are the opportunities. Outbound marketing consists mostly of feet on the street backed up by some printed collateral or media and you control that. You may have it both ways if you rent a building that provides a customer walk in environment and facilities for an outbound group.

Needs To Be A Contract Business

We see that building a business with recurring demand and necessity is a powerful model for longevity. This is made even stronger by putting your services under a contract.

Do you realize that every year, statistically speaking, 20% of your business is up for grabs, endangered by regular market churn—a competitor taking it, company closings, moves, downsizings, customers just don't like you anymore, or industries collapsing? The Yellow Pages is 10% out dated the day it arrives due to these factors and Internet data would be similar. Still, aside from business closings, if your customer is under contract he will make the effort to accommodate you even under these changing circumstances. If there is no contract then no need to bother. To make support services more stable put them under contract, annual or longer, even three years. This makes you less vulnerable to the 20% annual churn factor.

Contracts are just so vital. Contracts stabilize your business, help forecast revenues and provide lead time to adjust if the customer is canceling. If you have no contracts you can theoretically lose all your business in one month. Even a three-month contract is better than none.

Not having a contract likely means returning to the customer several times yearly to resell the deal. A contract relieves you of that and lets you put all that reselling time to better use. If I single out one *Small Business Survival 101* principle as most important to longevity it is selling via annual contract! If you cannot or will not do this then you have a business expiration date. If not selling things under contract then start. Most business owners speak of "building" a business and contracts are *something that you build upon.*

Sometimes an annual membership, offering perks, works in retail as a sort of contract. A television show sells annual memberships offering more detail on the news, sends it to you, and offers logo merchandise. Any shop could do similar. Small farmers have discovered contracts. Each week they deliver to households who sign for this service on a yearly basis. This makes it easier for them to judge future plantings and income. At the least, offer a loyalty program to better bond customers to you. If they have had five paid visits, give them the sixth free. Anything that helps them return to your business and take their eyes off the other guys will help secure repeat/return business.

Contracts should be written as "evergreen." This means they renew automatically yearly without re-signing. This is legal providing you give a 30 day out provision prior to the renewal date. If you customer is satisfied with you they are usually happy to let it renew which is just less hassle for you and them.

The diabetic testing supply business loves contracts. They will deliver them to your door free if you sign a yearly contract. And I am not making this one up but the Rid-X septic tank cleaner wants to mail you a box every month, under a yearly contract, to put into your toilet to keep your septic tank functional. My business has service contracts that allow me to plan my business better than just living on time and materials billing. The copiers we place are leased over a 36 to 60 month period. We try to write a service contract to cover the same period.

Contracts are important if you want to sell your business because a business with contracts is more valuable than one without them. Banks are examples of the power of contracts. The reason they are normally so stable is most everything they sell, like loans, are 36 -120 month contracts earning monthly profits. When one bank buys another they do so confidently because of the predictability provided by these contracts.

Contracts allow you to build in a methodical, predictable, and sound way. Picture an upside down pyramid with the point as your first contract. Each month you hope to add contracts which begins widening the upside down pyramid representing your growing customer base. Each year you hope to renew all existing contracts, which won't happen, and add new ones to widen the base. This stabilizes your business and grows it.

The most solid bases are onesey-twosey customers who do smaller amounts of business. They have the least turnover and provide the most stability. The larger the customer the more the potential instability. Contract customers facilitate relationship building, which helps renewals and provides fertile ground to offer ancillary contract services to grow business. Businesses without contracts rely on building goodwill, an accounting, and legal as well as practical term. Goodwill, the general goodness, patronization, and likeability built up in a business, is relied upon for repeat business but it is not as reliable as contract business.

You can put about any service under a contract if a business or consumer regularly requires it, so do so. Resist not requiring one because customers won't require you sooner than you think. A newcomer, a new offer, or a friend who is now in the business easily attracts away your customers. This will not happen if you have them under contract so why take this risk? You are protected. These contracts need to be non-cancellable which is what contracts are for—two parties agreeing to certain things in return for lower prices over an agreed time. Allow for small annual price increases of five per cent to provide for cost increases. After ten years a goal is having overhead covered, including owner pay, by contracted services that renew. Then hardware sales are clear profit. I have never quite gotten there but come close. I keep working on it.

I once had a fleet of copiers rented to a large firm. They renewed annually for nine years and were my largest account. I replaced old ones as needed which required a bank loan for equipment cost. Out of nowhere they canceled because of a corporate drop dead deal with another provider who would use them in their advertising. I was floored and sweating. They still had nine months and I counted on that revenue. I told them they were under contract and owed nine months. They tried to laugh it off and say they owed a month or two of liquidation. I had to produce the contract and climb the chain of authority, which got me my nine months of liquidation worth six figures. Whew! Thank you good contract.

Contract billing has the bonus of setting up a poor man's marketing effort. Send out paper invoices to contract customers because you can include advertising stuffers promoting products or special offers. This might be a discount coupon or announcing a new product. It could be a refrigerator magnet. The cost is little. Obtain the business emails of contacts so you can send email blasts periodically, which are also free. Most invoicing software allows printing special offers or promotional information on the invoice at no cost. Use color invoices.

B2B or B2C

Next, decide if you are going to be B2B or B2C? Hopefully you recognize these acronyms. Each requires a different focus for servicing the recurring demand. B2B means business selling to a business and B2C means business selling to consumer. You can do both but probably do best focusing on one. Either segment requires things like repairing, landscaping, mowing, delivery, cleaning, training, HVAC, Internet, tires, plumbing, computers, and all the rest. Advertising methods will be different. B2B nets bigger orders but B2C more orders. Free social media, such as YouTube and Facebook can drive people to your website at no cost to get exposure.

Social media techniques are more productive in B2C than in B2B but are still hit and miss and not a powerhouse. B2C has far more potential customers than the business market but businesses have quite a bit more buying power than any one consumer. Mass market advertising—TV, newspaper and radio—works well for the B2C market because it is a mass market. The B2B arena is not really a mass market and does not do as well with mass marketing methods. B2C marketing shoots with the massive spray of shotgun whereas B2B requires hunting with the more pinpoint accuracy of rifle. Ah yes, much to consider.

How To Grow Your Recurring Business

So now you have something going but what is the best way to grow it?

There are only five distinct ways to grow a small business and they are not complicated. That is not to say that they are easy to accomplish, they aren't, but there is not any mystery to what they are. No need to buy strategy sessions from gurus for the formulas nor a seven CD set that uncovers them. Neither will you need a working knowledge of how the space shuttle docks with the space station.

Here they are:

1. *Maintain sales to current customer base.* To add to your base the base cannot be going backwards which makes it that much harder to attain growth.

2. *Sell additional products to existing customers.* These would be new products sold to existing customers as you continue selling them your original products that address a separate need. This increases total purchases.

3. *Open a new sales territory.* Growth means increasing the ground you cover.

4. *Make an acquisition.* How to do this is in Chapter 4 but it means making a leveraged buyout of a competitor or a complimentary business.

5. *Secure new customers in existing territory.* That is self-explanatory.

These are the only growth strategies there are. Any others you hear in a different way will still fall under one of these headings. These headings sprout subheadings describing sales and marketing methods to accomplish them. Some of these are discussed in the chapter on selling. As I said, these are easier said than done but these are the strategies. It is well and good to get advice on executing them but ensure it is from someone who has grown a business doing them.

Alright, you just recovered the price of this book by saving you the price of a CD set or admission to a seminar on this subject. I do think it is worthwhile to spend money on courses and seminars if the subject matter is conducted by a sales and marketing expert .

The concepts in this chapter are vital for longevity. The hardest part might be spelling 'recurring' and making those growth strategies succeed! Change is coming though....fasten your seatbelt.

Moe's summation: "I like that we are a recurring necessity ourselves. We are glad to help the economy with your buying our recurring necessities like Frisbees, balls, bones, treats, food, sweaters, collars, leashes, toys, flea collars, tic medicine, grooming, bedding, travel kennels, water bowls and dog houses."

5 No Change...
...No Change

You are going along, making ends meet, making a bit of profit (?) and customers are sticking with you, then BLAM! Change strikes. More like BLAM! BLAM! BLAM! The Change Monster, Businessaurus Rex, is at the door wanting to devour your business. Be expecting it and be a bit in fear of it. Big, small, newly formed, or twenty years in business, change strikes like a lightning bolt.

Are you willing to change your business model? At some point you will have to. Hopefully you spot the need to do so while you have the time. Maybe it's adding something to it, taking something from it, replacing something, twisting it, turning it, burning it, baking it or breaking it. There is an old adage from somewhere that goes: *Don't try to push back the river.* From that came the more modern version : *Go with the flow.* Both are succinctly saying change is staring you in the face and find a way to change.

Let's see, not long ago Kodak made film, air mail was fast, TV cameras were huge, the only Internet was a phone, paper maps got you there, Korea only made rice, Wall St. and governments were too big to fail, China meant backward, real estate always went up, videos came from Blockbuster, Apple nearly went bankrupt, bank tellers gave you the cash, newspapers came in the driveway, TWA and Pan Am were class of the skies, books were bought in stores, a text was something written, phones were at home. You used to go to school to go to school but now distance learning means you don't have to while you earn a degree in your pajamas. High schools are replacing text books with convertible laptop computers. Now you bring your teacher a flash drive instead of an apple. Even the Internet is 25 years old.

The tech area is especially brutal with change. Watch sales declined because time is told by cell phones. Phones devastated photography and its aftermarket not to mention radios, landlines, camcorders, Mapquest, GPSs, alarm clocks, board games, cash, checks, and now laptop sales. Research In Motion, maker of the Blackberry, in only 2009 was named a top 100 fastest growing company, its smart phone deemed indispensible and called the Crackberry because so addictive, saw its stock plunge 90% from the impact of screen based phones. They fired 5,000 in 2012, one third of its workforce. If a well heeled, tech brained company like this has trouble....

We love new tech but each advance brings a death toll elsewhere. Indeed, the aim of most technological advances is to reduce the need for human participation. Nearly every passing year brings these changes maybe beginning with the Industrial Revolution. In 2012 Hewlett Packard fired 27,000 due to the hit taken by its computer and software business from the smart phone. Sharp Electronics is laying off 5,000. Electronics giant Panasonic fired 38,000 in 2011 after losses in its technology related businesses. This again shows the dangers of owning a technology based business, or, the dangers of unforeseen technology making you obsolete. The very nature of technology is planned obsolescence and change.

Manufacturing in the US has been considered on the decline for a while and killing off big cities. But wait! Made in the USA is making a change in the way of a comeback. Cheap US energy from shale and rising wages in China are making us more competitive. The unthinkable is happening with old factories re-opening. They will use fewer workers due to automation but still. Here we have sweet change of the good kind.

This decade saw the Great Recession, The Great Indebtedness, The Great Unemployment, The Great Oil Spill and The Great Corruption. There were Great Floods, Heat Waves, Volcanoes, droughts and a tsunami. The Brazilian rubber industry was decimated because a fungus ate it. All these changes impacted most businesses giving new meaning to The Greatest Generation. Must I go on? Just remember: "If things are bad they'll change. If things are good they'll change." To have long term business success deal with this bad boy. It is just not likely your business model today will be the same in five years or next year. Businesses have to accept more change than a vending machine.

Look around at the Gobbled and Gobblers who produce so much change. Gobblers gobble up smaller, less efficient businesses that brings a torrent of change to entrepreneurs which may save some from extinction but it changes everything. Amazon gobbled small book stores and the publishing business, Circuit City and now Best Buy. QVC did away with a few stores. We know what Apple products changed and know big banks gobble smaller ones until maybe there will only be One Big Bank. Small businesses are in the crosshairs of, or collateral damage of, the Gobblers. I guess it is survival of the fittest but hard on small businesses. Then again, it may turn out we are glad we are not one of these huge dinosaurs because a small business strength is its ability to change quickly where large ones are considerably more committed and fall hard too.

Bumper sticker: "If it has tires or testicles you are going to have trouble with it." Let's add having a business to that list. Trouble is the outcome of change that precedes it. Something flew out of its usual orbit and changed everything or at least something. Business ownership is a contact sport with things flying out of their normal orbits and putting you in contact with unexpected changes. You will contact all manner of adversity. There are competitors that want to beat you. Economies that want to bury you. Vendors that manipulate you. Bankers that may deny you. Employees who may deceive you. The main thing is to stay in contact. At times, be prepared to channel your inner Bruce Lee.

Be good at managing changes, all this trouble, and stay in contact with it to tame it. In a way, it is your constant companion. You sort of have to thrive on that. A business is a living breathing thing, a chameleon, always changing. Very little in business is forever which makes change a foe to take as seriously as an IRS inquiry. Remember five year plans? Right. Most of those are now one year. Companies that used to lease equipment now rent to stay quick on their feet. You frequently hear that Wall Street is 'spooked' because they feel that, for one reason or another, they do not know what the government, IRS, Congress, another country, blah, blah, blah, is going to do and how that will change their business. Cry us a river. We live there ourselves with much smaller checkbooks.

When I began one copier technician serviced 80 copiers and a good service record was one call every week. Then I had 18 technicians. Copiers continually became more reliable needing a call only every three months so now one technician services 300 machines! Technology changed things and I had to adjust. Technological changes can strike anywhere. Back when refrigeration became common ice block companies feared for their existence but quickly learned the new business of selling ice cubes. Right now canning companies are shaking because food producers are packaging into pouches that are cheaper than cans or bottles. All farmers are dealing with a 2012 unexpected drought over two thirds of the nation killing their year's business. And the beat goes on. Change, change, change. How do you best deal with change? You change. This removes you from your comfort zones.

Other changes are cultural and less brutal. Vocabulary like multitasking, download, instant messaging, tweeting, Facebook, email, blogs, iTunes, hits, e-books, voicemail, just-in-time delivery, and business casual did not exist 15 years ago. Each brought tidal change to the way people did things. This, in turn, affected existing businesses in a mostly negative way. Maybe yours.

"You deal with change by changing."

In 1999, when credit flowed, myself and a 50/50 partner secured an SBA loan for a corner lot and a new 12,000 square ft. building to house Kawasaki of Memphis. I still operated my office equipment dealership but this was an entrepreneurial dream. My partner operated day to day while I oversaw the financial. The facility was really nice and after three years in the top 15%. After eight years I wanted to cut back and sold my half. Ten months later a teenager, sitting in the showroom waiting for someone, got up, pulled a gun, and shot a salesman dead from behind. The bullet went through him and hit another. The shooter was 17, a gang member but the rest is unexplained, changing life forever for this business. Employees had distress and an armed guard was hired for $3500 a month. Eventually, the dealership closed. As sad and unpredictable as it gets and eight were jobless. Hard to see how this business X- factor could have been prevented.

Troubles and changes are financial, legal, moral, technological, HR, or governmental. Or 'other'. They could be partnership fallouts, embezzlement, lost accounts, the Great Recession, product obsolescence or lost passion. Trouble and change are interchangeable. If eight of ten things brought to you are not neutral to negative you are not getting the truth. A small business can be quite the calamity collection magnet. Murphy's Law—if it can go wrong it will—is out there! Let's try to get to a lot of truth in this chapter. I examine changes, troubles and hardships and show what might be done.

Everyone's situation is unique but creativity is the name of the deal-with-change- game and light bulb moments are needed. Never feel bad that some dam thing has befallen you. It likely has happened to everyone, it is just your turn. This is the nature of small business warfare and large. Take your banker, GM, AIG, Lehman Brothers, Chrysler or solar companies. They collected so much trouble that without a federal bailout they are not here. Did you get a bailout since you are a job engine of the economy?

Let's take a look at things in your power to help you deal.

The Worst Change-Losing Money

Hopefully it is a change. There is nothing worse than losing money because this threatens everything. I can take a lot but when red ink is stubborn that changes me. I get preoccupied, narrowly focused and even angry to fix it. This section is as serious as it gets but it is also going to be short. Why? Because there are only two strategies that work to change this change. One is to cost cut and the second is to get more business that is profitable.

There are important things to remember when cutting especially when it comes to employees. It is tempting to whack a $3000 monthly salary but it is not likely this is all net savings. Just about any employee contributes directly or indirectly to the bottom line. Cutting a person means effort somewhere is gone, some expertise, some customer relationship severed, some revenue, some muscle or cost containment skill is lost. This may mean savings are $1000-$2000 and not $3000. Maybe there are none at all. I find it better to ask for a company-wide 10% pay cut to save jobs and preserve company skills until profitability returns. It works and can contribute to better team camaraderie. My cutting rule is cut early and cut deep. Waiting too long is your fault and only makes it worse so take your pick. Cut enough so you don't have to do more again later which is demoralizing.

You can't cost cut your way to prosperity. It is no surprise that your second strategy then is to do more business of the profitable kind. You may need to raise a price or lower a price, cover more costs, replace a salesperson, add a salesperson, sell new products, make more sales calls, change your advertising, merge, make an acquisition, change comp plans to higher commission and lower salary, or, all of the above.

Winning Ugly

Businesses get sick just like people. It is just a matter of time. They may need medication, surgery or resuscitation. They might visit the emergency room a few times too, which is what this section is about. Emergency measures in this section are italicized. No, you won't find them taught in business school. This section could just as well be named "Watching Ways to Make Sausage." Some you wouldn't visit until the Great Recession munched cash flows and bottom lines. History may well term this period the Great Survival. Even before the GR maintaining positive cash flow was the number one problem for small business so now it is worse—more change and trouble—as few saw the GR coming. Then again, it may not be too different from all the other survival periods owners endure.

In 2010 there were 1.53 million bankruptcies, probably one near you and bankruptcy is a way of winning ugly. There were double the usual unemployed and everyone lost 30% on real estate. The country has negative net worth with debt of 17 trillion. Congress is continually gridlocked and dysfunctional. The biggest Wall St. firms, car companies and insurance giants failed or failed until bailed. Hard to paint an uglier picture. Ugly business conditions, yes? If they took out these behemoths, with their million dollar minds, imagine what the ugly effect is on small businesses.

Here's an ugly with my bank. I had *loans I wanted re-amortized* to save enough cash flow to not lay off two people. I thought that less damaging than ruining two lives. I met with the banks, talked nice and explained but they said no. I let them feel my displeasure and lagged on payment, 30 days late, 60 days late. They wanted another visit bringing a higher up. I said to return to timely payments they needed to heed my request. They countered with half which still did not get it done. I gave them an amortization schedule of how I was re-paying this re-amortized loan, whether they agreed or not. They relented. Ugly and stressful but worth it. Banks don't want your collateral or to write down a non-performing loan. Don't be afraid to press your case.

You probably have a few suppliers getting the majority of your money—a wholesaler, a landlord, a supplier. You are a valued customer hard to come by. When pressed *ask for extended terms or 25% off temporarily.* They won't be happy but will probably do it. With so much buying power having left the economy customers are the prize so realize you are one and have leverage. *Discover the power of asking.* A business CEO has the power and profitability of making requests. I have made calls to suppliers or customers to right some situation gone unprofitable. Such calls, for time spent, can be one of the most profitable things measured in return by the minute. There is money in negotiating and in asking! It is surprising how often those called respond favorably. Anyone working with you deserves payback.

Getting extended terms increases working capital. Don't feel bad about asking because, and I am not happy to say, Fortune 500 companies do it. I have two as customers and they purposely take 45 days to pay, our terms are net 10, and tell you so. That is 35 days past due. What to do? The same. *Everyone tries to make their numbers at the expense of the other guy's numbers!* Interestingly, one of these companies began a quick pay program paying, bless their hearts, our terms but for a 3% discount. We enrolled and get payment in seven days, worth it, but we shouldn't have to pay extra. This is just how it is in The Ugly Economy.

If you are faced with having to make a considerable expenditure like an office equipment, fork lift, direct mail campaign, insurance or many other things, *use Buyer Zone.* This is a site where you list what you in the market for and you will then get significant calls or bids from relevant vendors. It is going to get you down to about the cheapest street price.

For extra revenue Craigslist can *sell stuff you thought worthless.* I have sold thousands here, both business and personal, and it is all free. Nothing like extra cash for nothing. Each ad allows four pictures. Don't ask me how they make money. This site is so powerful it has collapsed want ads and hurt newspapers while helping consumer finances. It is better than eBay, especially for larger items because shipping is not an issue with all ads being local. You can use it to put an ad in a category advertising your business. Again for free.

Craigslist is a heavy traffic site and has a wide following so give it a go for more dough.

Another tactic is *bartering to pay bills*. If you have excess time and low cash but plenty of expertise or product ask to pay debt the old fashioned way—work it off! That is how 'trade' originated, buyer and seller literally traded. It works for both parties and each needs to use retail prices for the trade basis. Depending on your degree of desperation, the asking may take the form of telling. It's honorable.

Be cheap. Look for good deals on used things. Buy used cars. The days of spending to make yourself look good are over. Have employees and family be cheapn' like parakeets, tighter than jeans from the dryer! Hold working capital with a vise grip. Think along the lines of removing every other light bulb and turning off the hot water heater. Stop short of unplugging the clocks before you go home though.

You can *lag on payroll taxes and sales taxes* for even three months. You get penalized and have to catch up, but it's a short term loan. On non-government stuff, after 90 days, expect to hear from a lawyer or bill collector. That being said, they are quite busy these days and it takes longer to get serious. All of this hurts credit scores but you were probably not planning major purchases or loan requests anytime soon. My company sells to doctors helping them go paperless and implement electronic records. We sold two practices at $50,000 each. To my complete shock they were declined financing for poor credit. One doctor had a score of 500 and another 400. Talk about ugly. Sign of the times.

If you owe an out of state company it is much more expensive for them to come after you than an in state vendor. The out of state company must hire a local attorney and the case has to be heard locally. From what I have seen, out of state firms will not do this for deals under maybe $10,000. They tend to hassle you a while then write them off. You may still get hammered with collection calls but until served papers nothing serious happens although a repo man will take a vehicle. Collateral of wicker baskets, end tables, or pumps may be collateral for someone but are not likely to be actioned because they are not very marketable.

Chapter 11

Should it become too much maybe *filing Chapter 11* bankruptcy gets you re-righted. That is what it is for and Chapter 11 reorganization is the business owner's friend. It is a shame it has the word bankruptcy attached because it is about continuing instead of closing as in Chapter 7. The day you file begins an automatic stay that causes all creditors, collectors or court actions to cease during this time which may run twelve months. This time is for forming new plans with creditors, you are protected from nearly all collection/court efforts including the IRS for back taxes. Another benefit is that you do not pay on most of your debt during this time to build working capital. The bankruptcy court, a Federal court, discharges some debt outright, usually unsecured creditors, and partially discharges secured debt providing the secured parties agree. The amount that remains for you to pay, with terms, is usually equal to the value of collateral.

Bankruptcy attorney fees are $25,000 with at least half up front. Chapter 11 works best if you are having problems servicing debt that has become too much. It is a different story if you just cannot cover operating overhead which means Chapter 7 liquidation. Chapter 11 cannot discharge past due sales taxes, income taxes and payroll taxes but they do go into the reorganized plan to be paid over 60 months. In the automatic stay no further penalties or interest accrue either. During the stay, you must pay current taxes and keep them current. Chapter 11 filings have a strong chance of helping you recover if your business model is viable after this combination of discharging unsecured creditors and reworking secured ones.

Be mindful if you discharge unsecured debt of important suppliers you may not be supplied again which could shut you. Statistics say only one in ten businesses come through a Chapter 11 but that is because many are dead on arrival and not that the process is ineffective. There is a new twist for clients needing Chapter 11 reorganization bankruptcy but can't afford one called a managed chapter 11. The attorney visits the client's vendors, a welcome relief for the client, and explains his client is chapter 11 bound and tries to renegotiate the debt without court. It is less drastic than Chapter 7 though more expensive. So there may be a new chapter in your life, Chapter 11 (gallows humor).

Winning Ugly can be ugly but not as ugly as losing all. Bankruptcy filings are, unfortunately, common. Dave Ramsey, the nationally syndicated radio host on thrift, has. Chapter 11 filing is a temporary measure and you have to bring yourself back at some point. Every business has something ugly they are not proud of. Be willing to play hardball, be determined, be smart, and live to play another day. Moving now to a more positive mode, let's look at ways to rise and regain some swagger!

Fight or Flight?

When adversity strikes a small business owner he needs to figure out where to best allocate his brain neurons. They are his best weapons if he can keep them on the boil. But conflicts with vendors, bankers, government agencies, employees, or whoever, can seriously threaten the emotional reserve. It may be of some comfort for the owner to know that everyone has their share of trouble no matter how big they are. You opponent goes through a sorting out process himself of who he wants to fight and how far he wants to go with it. This can be a judgment call based upon the fight, or lack of it, seen in their opponent, you the business owner. It is that kind of world.It pays to put up a robust resistance to something seriously threatening you. It need not cost much. They just need to really see it in you. I tell my vice-president that 95% of the time you can be yourself managing a business but 5% of the time you have to be willing to bare a switchblade from your shoe and show your adversary you mean business. This means that they see, feel and hear your considerable resolve. This costs nothing but it can't be faked either. If you ever watched the "Rocky" movies then this means they see your Eye of the Tiger. Sometimes the 5% battle, if lost, can turn the other 95% and we don't want that. What you do want is to try and avoid a serious and expensive battle in the first place. Maybe just buying needed time is the victory.

I hope you get what I am saying. If not, I checked with my dog Moe to see if there is a Moe Lesson on this. There is and it may be one of his best. Moe knows threats, how to handle them and possesses considerable courage. He lives on acreage with a horse and a donkey, neither of which like him and he does not care for them either. Moe is a gimpy shelter rescue dog who can't run very fast. Be that as it may, Moe feels it is his world out there and the 1000 pound horse and 500 pound donkey need to get the heck out based upon his 50 pound say so. Moe once ventured into the horse pasture to tell Chief (horse) how it was. Chief promptly lifted his hind leg and sent Moe 20 feet in the air which somehow did not hurt him. You would think that would be enough to stop him but it isn't.

When Chief and Dusty are in range Moe still wanders over, squares his shoulders at the imposing monsters, bares his teeth, folds back his ears, and lets fly a very angry sounding bark-a-thon. It can be just enough to stop the monster pair and hold off Armageddon by a whisker. Moe does this by planting sufficient doubt in their minds that his teeth may take a bite out of their legs so they think better of it and wander away as Moe stands down with victory. They do see the much smaller physical threat in front of them but all his noise and bluster is taking up a much larger space in their brain cavity. They know they can whip Moe but don't want to allocate the time fighting him today, nor risk a bite, and decide on better use of their talents besides tussling with such a single minded dog. It could work out like that with your adversary too.

Somebody's Coming After Me!

There will be troubling times when discussions with some 'adversary' break down. The next step may be a lawsuit, an audit, or a collection effort. You may or may not be guilty as charged. It can be intimidating, distracting and expensive. Remember that your opponent feels the same. The first rule of this kind of combat is to "make them work hard for it." The legal system greatly favors the defendant in terms of time. It can easily take a year for your case to conclude in court. Throw all the delay tactics out there available in hopes this eventually breaks the will of your opponent causing him to cease or settle.

Do not take the "I just want to get this over with" position because that is the expensive position. Not that lawyers are cheap either but if they are just filing motions with the court that is only a fax. You ask for continuances, more time to get the information, to accommodate a witness, or accommodate a deposition. This can go on and on even into multiple years. Keep in mind that attorneys do not get paid much for filing motions. Their payday is defending you in a trial. Thus they may try to hurry. Stay in charge when you hire an attorney and don't be afraid to question any fees.

Bill collectors sending horrible letters and harassing phone calls work mostly through these intimidation tactics. If you will just wait them out, ignore their threats, you will see the amount they seek drop and drop. Bill collectors cannot take you to court. Only the creditor can. If the creditor has turned you over to a collection agency it is a good sign he is not taking you to court.

If you have some agency coming in for an audit you go through the delay tactics too. Provide limited information that requires them to dig through it. Don't provide nice accommodations but rather cramped ones and maybe the AC is not working. In most audits it is not advisable for the owner to be the contact point. Assign someone and leave yourself free to hear what was said to the contact and give yourself time to formulate your defense.

The make-them-work-hard-for it tactic will almost always save you money, buy you time, break the other guy's will and allow you space to calm down. Patience is your ally.

Make an Acquisition

My business suffered a Great Recession drop in top line and employee attrition. That is change, for sure, and not for the better. Neither sat well with me and I hate them. I have been hungry to remedy that and selling more stuff has, so far, fallen short. Making an acquisition is one way to increase top line, gain customers, new expertise, positive cash flow and further solidify your fortress. Sound too good to be true? It's not. I kept thinking there must be small computer network companies in a similar boat trying to return to more positive, proactive business plans rather than just coping. I could see how bringing one into my fold would be compatible, and help both, so I hunted one under five employees.

I called the yellow pages talking to owners and a few got follow up meetings. Strangely enough, while walking around my building, I saw such a company and went in. It looked sparse, no receptionist, and empty desks. I thought this looks perfect. The owner was there and we talked and eventually made a deal after a few months—one anyone could—if two owners are of the same mind. The deal, of which I am purchaser, nets two technicians and the owner who will help me grow it. The business they bring pays all their expenses. They shed expenses such as rent, insurance, phone, bookkeeper, and dropped one person for further savings. We split the savings and from my part, which is money from the combined savings and not my pocket. It's addition by subtraction. I pay a term payment for the purchase. I get new expertise, top line and new mojo.

The acquired company gets my customer base to sell to and takes advantage of those established relationships. By coming into my company the owner is freed of admin duties and has time to focus on growth. The definition of a good deal is one good for both parties and this is one of those. Take that Change Monster! All paid by a monthly payment from new positive cash flow from the get together. No bank borrowing. This is a great solution to bad changes in the economy. A change for the better! You can do the same targeting small operations that might do similar for you. You can do more than one as you solidify each one first.

1+1=3

The guiding formula in an acquisition is one plus one equals three. This means two companies together produce something greater than the two standing separately that is more profitable. This accelerates growth and has the advantage of buying something known. You have to work to keep it there but in one swoop you buy up new business that would've taken years to obtain sale by sale. My CPA puts it this way: buy positive cash flow. The savings from the combined companies, after debt service, must produce positive cash flow.

How do you go about buying another company? The business logic of it is up to the two parties. The due diligence, which comes next, is up to the buyer. Conducting due diligence is the process that verifies you are getting what is represented. First, get three years tax returns of the owner and the business. Next, get the sales tax returns of the business which verifies revenues (taxable ones). Next have your accountant audit the company's banks statements for the past year. Finally, get the past three years financial statements on the company. Make sure one year balances into the other. All this should be enough to verify revenue and expenses. Do a UCC search on any property you are buying to ensure it is free of liens.

Large companies getting larger do a lot of this. For example, Fuji Films made 40 acquisitions to shore up losses in film. Walgreens spent 7 billion buying a chain in England to grow there. Salesforce went public in 1999 for 110 million dollars used mostly to buy 21 companies. Now you know how big companies get bigger. You are not looking at this kind of money but at this strategy. For the business owner there is long term debt for the acquired business so this is long term strategy. An acquisition, also called a leveraged buyout, works best if one moves in with the other since it is hard to get savings standing separately. Very key to this working is the owners are compatible. This is not the easiest thing—two owners agreeing—but refrain from criticism and focus on the new good stuff you two are going to do and how it improves things for each.

The new business mass and economy of scale an acquisition brings provides new cushion to cut from should you need to downsize. If you are already lean as can be then further downturns bring unmanageable pain so you are vulnerable. Although it would not be the primary reason to acquire a business the new business should provide this reserve to cut back whereas there was none pre-acquisition.

Diversify

Do more than one thing! Diversifying is a way to deal with change before change deals with you. More than one iron in the fire, more than one way to skin a cat, full magazine in the gun, four wheel drive, walking and chewing gum, able to play golf and baseball. You get it. By growing your business by new markets or products within an already successful business you become an intrapreneur, the highest rung on the entrepreneurial career path. Acquisitions accomplish this—hedge against future change by acquiring new capability instead of developing it. If one area has a downturn you have another to pursue. Hopefully the new firm has new competencies for you and new revenue sources. Large companies make acquisitions primarily for this reason—to enter new markets. For example I bet you didn't know Arm and Hammer Baking Soda bought Trojan Condoms. Highly doubtful those two markets would tank at the same time and condoms are considered a recurring necessity.

If you don't diversify by buying do it by learning. Learn to sell a new product to existing customers. Diversifying is a basic business strategy long used to hedge against change and as a way to grow. Kroger is beginning to sell clothes to its food customers who, of course, also need clothes. Take that Target, who used to sell only clothes but went to selling groceries to its clothing customers. Let's face it, it is harder to get new customers than reselling to existing ones. So find a new offering to sell existing customers and, if successful, you theoretically double business if each bought one. Do it slowly and have a few close customers pilot it as beta testers.

To successfully implement a new product the effort needs to be led by a *champion*. This is a person, and it could be you, that has expertise and passion in the area and champions its mission. Starting a new revenue area is like starting a business but without putting in infrastructure. A champion may have to be stolen from a competitor or you may need a headhunter to locate one. The right champion is everything and you should not scrimp here if you want success. If you don't diversify with a new product do it by taking on a new territory.

Go where you have not gone. Hire a salesperson to cover it. Diversify your own orbit and circulate in new groups. Join a new organization, go to chamber meetings, take a leadership role in a group, whatever causes you to meet new people.

Law Of The Pinball

I have a term, The Law Of The Pinball, my jargon for taking diversifying action. You remember the pinball machine that took flippers and body English to keep the pinball in play. You may have been a Pinball Wizard yourself. The longer in play the more likely the pinball hits something, and then another something and so on, that lit for a score. Same for you. Get in play and bounce around until hitting something for a score. One thing leads to another.

Christopher Columbus set out on a regular cruise only to discover America. Steve Jobs cobbled together a computer in his garage which led to today's iMania. My daughter volunteered for a mission trip and two years later runs her own mission company. It expanded into a business that sells women's accessory necklaces and bracelets nationwide made in the mission countries.

Pfizer set out to make a heart drug called Viagra. Testing found it also did something else. Bing! Bing! Bang! Bang! Cling Clang! The result was unexpected but made Viagra a best-selling drug. Vending company Coinstar discovered a business taking people's change and put machines everywhere. After a few years learning that environment they pinballed out a vending machine called Red Box which now accounts for 85% of revenues. A new Red Box is placed every minute. I have told of a visit to a company to look at its product line. I noticed their many water jug stations and as a result, Bing! Bing! Bang! Bang! Cling Clang! I made a large sale of a competing product. Any kind of prospecting puts the pinball in play and this sale would not be had I not been moving around.

My company sells to doctors and from that became aware of a government program that rebated $40,000 for implementing electronic records. The paperwork was daunting and time consuming so doctors didn't file it and let the money go. I pinballed my company into being their filing service. I have girls that push paper and do detail so we ramped up on the required documentation. It is a one-time thing but we charged 10% and earned $50,000 and the doc got his rebate. I hadn't done anything like that but the point is I encountered this opportunity bouncing off another. I have technicians who regularly service business computers. They get asked by customers and employees how to do things that they do not understand. That is common. Most of us know some things and nothing about others so I ran an inexpensive ad in my church bulletin saying call the "Computer Tutor" who will come help you with software instruction. I have the expertise in house but just pinballed it to new customers and obtained new business.

To pinball well back away from business and attend trade shows that percolate creativity. I do this every few years and always pinballed into something. Once it was a seminar on copier technicians becoming printer technicians since printers are baby copiers. Bingo. Did that and picked up new service/supply business from these eaters and drinkers. At another show a drinking water company exhibited jugless water coolers. "This is a piece of office equipment" I thought. I took it to current customers and new ones selling hundreds. I would not have entered either new market without pinballing to somewhere that stimulated new thought. There will be no score, bells clinging nor bright lights flashing, if the ball (you) is not put in play! The motion is the thing. "Changing on a dime" is an agility small business CEOs will beat the pants off Fortune 500 CEOs. They just cannot change very fast while you can enter a new market in a week. Get the ball rolling! BING! BING! BING! I should list Law of The Pinball as one of the P Laws in the leadership chapter.

Keep Commitments Short

IBM had a rental program for copiers more expensive than a lease which I thought strange—a large company renting something they would have for years. Then again, IBM rented buildings and had temporary employees. This was a company with money so what's up with that? It was because they worry about the Change Monster too. All this temporary commitment let them *quickly* jettison expenses and for good reason it turns out. IBM was famous for Selectric typewriters, word processors, copiers, dictation equipment and personal computers. Today, they do not make any of these which altered facility and employment needs that they were ready for.

Keep lease space to three years and don't buy the building. Hire part time people. Rent stuff. If you buy something consider a used one. A lot of gear and equipment is underused and has surprising life left for a lot less dough. All this keeps you from getting hung out if things turn. You can dump overhead quick enough that it does not strangle you, a proactive strategy against the Change Monster. Know change is coming and try not to resist it. Read it quickly and make adjustments. Get in front of it. Make your business moves with it always in mind because it is a formidable adversary. Read *Who Moved My Cheese,* a 96 pager that sold many based upon dealing with change.

Another driver of shorter commitments is Congressional gridlock. Its bipolar nature keeps long term measures from passing which casts businesses into similar short term, guarded thinking. Congress has gone to one year extensions. Lower tax rates expire in one year or some funding is scheduled to be withdrawn in a year etc. This crimps businesses from making longer term commitments because they don't know what changes are coming or what changes to make.

Counterpunch!

Most big problems requiring change begin as neglected small ones. You may over eat a while, then a while longer, then forego exercise and before long you are overweight. You may neglect tire pressures only to wear them out earlier, only to cost you more in gas, and then misalignment leading to premature bearing wear and larger expense. Either problem chain is easily checked if one desires. Cut back food intake the next day and exercise some. Put some air in the tires. But folks still don't because we have met the enemy and it is ourselves. Too often it takes a major mental whack to make us take the needed action. Same goes running a business. You let smaller problems pass without correction. Maybe you indulged in too many discounts or lagged on collections. You let price increases from vendors go unchallenged or allowed employee tardiness hurting customer response time. Slow moving inventory has gathered. Your website needs updating. Just the nuts and bolts of running a business with the small forces of change trying to worm into your business and cause trouble. Have your owner's eye on this stuff and if something gets amiss COUNTER PUNCH meaning take action *right now,* not later I may raise a price, cancel the rug cleaning service, donate an obsolete product to bring in service, send a tech to collect the check, fine a slow employee, ask a vendor for a better price, and delegate the task of solving anything else ASAP. So counter punching is a discipline to prevent the Change Monster from getting a foothold. There is that word discipline again, so key to success. Owners love their independence, but still need a boss, so think of counter punching as that boss that screams this each time there is a new negative: " Do something now!" I know you don't like anyone telling you what to do but if it is Your Own Greatness you can accept it. Don't let the great freedom of bosshood lull you from the discipline it takes to stay in business.

Bold Changes

It could even be a bottom line or the bottom line of this whole book. The fact of the matter is that leaders frequently need to bring about bold changes. These are out of the box moves requiring risk above your comfort zone. Maybe it is giving a presentation to an influential group that scares you to death. Maybe it is stepping out with a new product you are not sure of. Could be you want to open in a new city. Maybe it is implementing a hopeful marketing campaign. How about trying to secure an appointment with someone out of your league?

Other changes may be firing the bottom ten percent, plotting ways to appear on television, attempting to acquire someone or finally making an important decision. None are expensive, mostly require extra gut, but bold initiatives yield bold results. They can also yield zero but the added costs for the attempts is small so you are not out much. If a true entrepreneur you are supposed to create boldly anyway, it is part of the job. We know you are busy being busy but take time for a few bold initiatives.

I just never see, aside from sheer luck, real progress being made in a business if the owner is not stepping out there. By this I do not, by any means, mean he is risking the company at every move. I do mean that he is boldly leading his team in a driven, inspired, and time optimized way, some good data in hand, to obtain the needed results. He is not sitting behind a desk, behind a closed door, nor invisible on the battle field, not in contact with customers, and still expecting improved results. No. He sets objectives, creates sense of urgency, maximizes productivity, puts in the time, chops wood, exhorts his team, is in the field with them, and THEN can expect changes.

Small Changes

Some days you are the pigeon and some the statue, some days the bug and other days the windshield. Here are pigeon and bug events with possible solutions. These are 'regular' changes and 'X factors', not life threatening but cause trouble. Expect these more than the more brutal conditions we discussed. Here are some with possible solutions:

- An employee has a drug, alcohol or legal problem: *Help them once if they are cooperating.*
- You have to fire someone: *If you are sure, sooner is always better than later.*
- There has been a burglary: *you carry insurance, right?*
- There has been an embezzlement: *same thing.*
- A disgruntled salesperson left with customer lists: *you can go to court and usually get an injunction preventing calling on existing customers.*
- Construction is going on in front of your business: *talk to mayor or city engineer for any help.*

- You are to be audited for some tax: *never attend it yourself. Your accountant can and should do it.*
- The Internet has started selling your product: *the Internet can't do service and customer service work.*
- You can't keep the people you need and can't pay more: *max out non-cash benefits.*
- You have to hire someone with certain skills: *use Monster or Career Builder online search of resumes for about $500.*
- Your costs of doing business keep increasing: *raise your prices a bit to help neutralize them.*
- Your business area is deteriorating: *start looking around.*
- Stress has been getting the best of you: *begin cardio exercise.*
- Physical inventory shows significant shrinkage: *you have theft going on or bad accounting.*
- You are being sued: *small claims court cases (usually under $15,000) heard in months. Appeal to higher court. Higher courts may take a year to hear. Usually can get one continuance. Take it. In about two years there will be a verdict.*
- Not making a profit: *fire yourself. Kidding. Can cost cut some but must increase sales at some point.*
- Key employee falls ill: *accommodate at all costs and divvy up duties. Consider buying Key Man Insurance.*
- Business falls into a slump and is threatened: *reduce company pay 5-10% across the board. Restore when things improve. Commence a telemarketing or direct mail campaign to get leads.*

Most business problems have simple solutions, they are just difficult to execute. "I need to hire a good sales person." Easy to conclude but hard to find. "I need to increase the margin". Raising the price is easy but will you lose customers? "I need to reduce my overhead." Absolutely, but what will hurt and what won't? I recommend, tongue in cheek, to visit ehow.com for a way to do something. They have quite a directory on how to accomplish many things. There is always something that can be done. There is. That does not mean you know what it is. It does mean you have to find out what it is.

Change seems to come most often as Frankenstein but can also be the Good Tooth Fairy. You land the big account, hire the right people, get a new product line, get certified in some new skill, open a new sales territory or come up with a great marketing campaign that works. Rather than letting change hit you it is best if you strike first. My wife is a counselor and has this sign in her office: "No change...no change." So true. Periodically, most businesses have to change their model to stay competitive because no business model lasts forever. Any way you look at it change is your bedfellow. List it as an expense item on your income statement—allowance for change—to stay reminded of its presence and that it carries costs which is just part of the business of business.

Consider this by Portia Nelson on navigating change.

1. "I walk down the street. There is a deep hole in the sidewalk. I fall in. I feel helpless. It isn't my fault. It takes forever to find my way out."
2. "I walk down the street. There is a deep hole in the sidewalk. I pretend I don't see it. I fall again. I can't believe I am in the same place. It isn't my fault. It takes a long time to get out."
3. "I walk down the same street. There is a deep hole in the sidewalk. I pretend I don't see it. I fall in. It's a habit. My eyes are open. I know where I am. It's my fault. I get out immediately."
4. "I walk down the same street. There is a deep hole in the sidewalk. I walk around it."
5. "I walk down a DIFFERENT street!"

There is a song we all know, something like "....a change is gonna do ya good." Maybe, maybe not. But it is going to do ya somehow. Take heart though, you can conquer all by being the person in the next chapter.

Moe's summation: "This is where humans are better. Dogs hate changes. We do not like our naps, meal time, or play time changed. We are creatures of habit and it serves us. Then again, we don't run businesses and this is probably why."

6

The Leader
Gets It Right

E very organization can be made better or worse depending on its leader. As an employer, whether just you and a few or a bunch of followers, success depends upon you. Period. It does not depend on you doing everything. It just depends on you.

Are leaders made or born? Yes. The overwhelming opinion anymore is they are made. Don't confuse being a boss with being a leader either. Being the boss just means something gave you authority whereas being an effective leader means you carry authority. Good to be both!

By definition leaders are found out front, literally, as in motivating a group and figuratively as in designing strategy. Whatever you plan will have unpopular pain because the necessity for leadership implies there are things to be overcome. Think of effective leaders like Moses, Patton, Churchill, Eisenhower, Martin Luther King, George Washington, Lincoln, Vince Lombardi, Gandhi, and most parents. Fred Smith, FedEx founder says "leadership is both something you do and something you are." A long time ago Confucius summed up how to be an effective leader: *"Tell me and I forget. Show me and I remember. Involve me and I will understand."* Amen.

Leaders only have three missions. That's all. They are: get things done, stand for things like goals, and delegate. The problem is under 'get things done' are 500 things such as morale building and….and…. and… The 'stand for things' section is simpler but vital. It's your philosophy. Employees should be able to recite what you stand for as well as your directives on doing the job right. They are beliefs everyone buys into. Delegating is fun—getting subordinates to do the work and, importantly, the right ones. Now you are getting things done through others which is the definition of management.

Leadership is such a vital element in the success of a company. Some of it can be learned and some can't. And sometimes it means you are careful not to fall on your own sword. There are plenty of leaders run amok from sword mishandles that cost dearly like presidents Nixon or Clinton, various generals or congressmen, or an ego obsessed CEO that crossed one too many lines.

"Where there is no vision people perish."

You are not attempting to lead a nation or a professional team although you could after leading a small business. I will hone leadership to what it means in our position: everything. It means you get it done and you get it right, no excuses. There will be excuses for why things may not have gone right, sure, you just cannot accept them because you have to get it done or perish. The late Steve Jobs has a good story about this. He meets with new vice-presidents and tells them the difference between them and the janitors. He says that if a janitor explains why an area is not clean he accepts their excuse but at VP level excuses are not accepted.

Since you cannot do all the work, you hire employees, have vendors, customers and contractors. They look to you for inspiration, direction, payment and one who attains success so they do too. No pressure.

Something humbling is remembering tremendous leaders like Jobs, Bill Gates Warren Buffet, and Fred Smith had the same 24 hours we do. They went global and we hope to get beyond the county line. All had to sleep and are married with kids. Before I owned my business I had never been a leader, maybe a line leader in grade school. I was a good salesperson so I could talk and conduct myself but usually felt uncomfortable in front of a group. When we started there were three of us and I was not the majority nor the leader. I was the sales guy. In short order our leader did not want to be and asked me to buy him out. I was reluctant, actually, and one reason was I would have to lead. Selling was good because I mainly had to lead myself but my mix of ten people scared me. Do I really want to take THAT on? People have a bunch of trouble, illness, needs, moods, kids, disagreements, divorces and what not. They want more money, cheap medical, breaks, and less work. Most did not like sales types like me.

I thought my troubles were over when five banks turned down requests to buy the majority. Phew! That settles that, I thought. Then one called that would loan half the request. The majority guy really wanted out because he took it if I signed a note for the rest so I did. Now I was a leader of some kind. Next I did what any leader would—call a meeting! I asked what everyone thought and there was not much response. Brother. I told them I liked the business, knew office equipment, and liked the independence of our mission. Being religious I said this is what God wanted and I promised fun which they liked better than anything I said.

Honesty is good, and a major leadership element, so at least I hit that target. I spent most days still selling, bringing in money. Machines sold and once in a while we hired another technician. We grew and it was feeling pretty cool to me. I began taking everyone to lunch and sometimes closing at 4:00 for Happy Hour since I promised fun. Somewhere in there smiles came and a relaxed manner extended towards me. Heck, we liked each other. That is what was working for us. This moved me a great deal emotionally because they were counting on me and believing in me and that really dialed up my game. They could be anywhere but chose here. From then on, I felt I worked for them instead of the other way around while I enjoyed being a meaningful person in their lives. The leadership role produced a new and powerful motivation. I responded to it. I liked it. I grew into it.

I kept selling, where I felt my worth laid, but with 15 employees things were poorly run inside and it was time to become, ahem, more presidential and less salesman so I hired a sales manager. Boy, was I bored. The employees liked it, though, and I brought needed improvements. I worked closely with the sales manager to make sales. I had more time than I used to but greatly enjoyed going around barbing with everyone. I planned company picnics, bowling nights, awards banquets, go kart nights, softball teams, made people plaques, took people to lunch, wrote a company newsletter, told everyone how great they were, and we prospered. I produced happy motivated people. I helped with personal stuff sometimes loaning a bit of money. I loved all that and it is personally fulfilling. I never had to worry about employee turnover.

In 1994 I got nominated for Small Business Executive of the Year out of 200 in Memphis. About 1000 business people came to the hotel ballroom where the winner would be announced. It was rather formal but when they called my name my folks went nuts. They grabbed me, yelled, tasseled my hair and made my tie crooked. When I got to the podium I looked like I had been on a bender. The MC said : "Tom, I just wish your people would get behind you." I knew then I had become something more valuable than a salesperson and a real leader. It was more powerful and more profitable than bagging sales. There was a lot going on there that I am glad to now put on paper. Let's see what was working besides my conviviality.

Treat Everyone Differently

The simple premise behind this is that we are individuals and do best when treated as such so I find the most effective leadership element for a small business owner is *treating everyone differently*. None of us come with an owner's manual. I think this philosophy is a unique ability of a small business and a key to its success. I know it works because it is what

I've done for three decades. This does not mean everyone is not treated fairly, just differently.

How effective is it to motivate a 29 year old mother of two in sales with the same techniques for a 40 year old divorced technician? Not very. I worked schedules so mothers could pick up kids from school if she started earlier in the day and then go home. Let me just say this. If you do anything to help a working mother get mother time you never need to do another thing for her. It moves them. Would doing this for my 40 year old technician mean anything? No. See what I am saying? However, he was a golf freak and loved golf outings. If he had one I let him off Fridays at noon and not count as vacation. The reaction was not as strong as the mother's but, well, you get the idea.

I look for opportunities to do these things. It makes for grateful, motivated employees and I get satisfaction adding to someone's life. I have some lifestyle adjustment for everyone so, in that sense, all are treated equally. The across the board equality approach is for lazy leaders who like spelling out rules and having them followed. I doubt the words fun or motivation or flexibility are in any such book nor produce anything but mediocre clock watchers.

My leadership method is being an Employee Godfather—I give tailor-made favors. Many, like extra time off, don't cost much. It really just duplicates what it takes to sell successfully to an array of customers. You find their needs and satisfy them or find their problem and give a solution. Here are some inexpensive Employee Godfather things:

- Let employees use company assets like the truck or warehouse to store something. If you have old stuff no longer used, like a workbench, vacuum, chair, table, tool, file cabinet, desk, give them to employees.
- Allow employees to barter company products to help them with personal purchases. Say they need a new air conditioner. They can barter away the profit on a copier to give the air conditioning company but have to pay the actual cost.

- Help employees with the deductible for a hospital stay. Employees each agree to chip in, say $50, to pay the person's deductible. Company pays any shortage.
- Work out flex time to make for better commutes or work schedules. Maybe let some work from home at times.
- Have skeleton days. On a long weekend, or slow business period, send everyone home with pay but have a few stay so things can stay open.
- Give a Movie Day. Awesome. It is for inside people who never get out. Outside people come in and hold down things for the insiders to have a lunch and a movie. Cheap. They talk about it forever.
- Hold pot luck luncheons monthly. Employees cook and bring it. Does not sound like much but the camaraderie of sharing cooking is amazing. You buy the drinks. Play company trivia at it asking questions about the company giving $5 for each right answer. Wrong answer means money carries over.
- Recognize great efforts on a monthly and yearly basis. Nice plaques do this, cash awards, use of company car for a year, parking spot with a name, recognition of any kind.
- Have a company bowling night even if people don't bowl. Bowling allies have versions for this like Wacky Bowling.

Work FOR your employees which is known as servant leadership. It is fun, it reduces tension and centers around the leader removing barriers to productivity including psychological ones. He guides more than bosses. You did realize you had to be a psychologist, right? When in tune with employees you are at your best and they play hard for you. For a mental image picture a team in a huddle, shoulder to shoulder, arm in arm, listening to its leader call plays and then going all out to make them work. When there is disharmony, bad leadership, uncaring attitudes, or bad apples, when the leader tries calling a play employees mentally look like a breaking huddle—everyone going in a different direction.

By treating employees differently, based upon individual needs, you instill pride of ownership in the company by forming things around *them*. You would agree nobody ever washed a rental car because there is no pride of ownership. Leaders need to instill this pride among the employees—a mental equity. When people feel pride they buff, wax, cheer, promote and defend something and you want that something to be your company. They won't own it but fans do not own the Green Bay Packers either but still support and feel a part of them. This pride flows through employees in efforts and representations to customers resulting in more business. Morale will be high and carry you through low times too. What kind of car are you driving? Not a rental, of course.

Goal Setting

Maybe nothing is more important than this one. The leader has to get it right and the financial ones come first. To get everyone sticking with them could well be the most important thing to business survival. Maybe these goal are best labeled "standards of survival". As humans, we know what our bodily standards are supposed to be if we want to live. Cholesterol, blood pressure, blood glucose and all the rest need to be at a certain level to live a while. The medical community does not lower them based upon how hard they are to attain. In football you must go 100 yards to earn six points. Changing this to 90 yards because it is very cold or rainy or whatever won't happen. There are similar financial benchmarks that apply to your business that you set, or that set themselves, after you have set other stuff. The main thing here, is that it is you as leader doing or deciding these settings. They have to be right. You don't want to be setting your business end zone at 85 when it is 115.

This is harder than it seems. One problem of being the boss is you have no boss. Well, so to speak. If not making the necessary goals you may excuse yourself for a time, explain it away, or take sympathy with some non-performing employee who is impacting this. These are understandable behaviors but can prove deadly if indulged too long. Do it like any parent constantly setting the boundaries of acceptable behavior for a child or when training pets. The leadership point is not wavering on critical standards and to form company efforts to meet them. What you do not want is to say "well, here is what we seem to be able to do so that will be our standard."

> "*The first responsibility of a leader is to define reality. The last is to say thank you. In between the two the leader must become a servant and a debtor. That sums up the progress of an artful leader.*"
> —Max DePree

Ego Is Expensive

Business owners, especially males, possess large egos second to NBA players and politicians. It is sometimes called *hubris*. Ego, at least on display, is not a good thing in leadership but shouldn't be confused with self confidence which is a good thing. I have seen seriously destructive things happen to owners exercising egos, some the equivalent of falling on their sword. Do we doubt the Wall Street collapse had, as a root, CEOs on ego binges? Nothing but financial bloodshed went down there.

In a small business you can mess up just as bad flexing your ego neurons. Maybe you insist on bringing your three dogs to work or posturing in front of employees, or being sloppy with the example you set. Only you can correct that and too many indulgences can bring down your company. I really like management guru Peter Drucker's comment that is pertinent here: "*Charisma becomes the undoing of leaders. It makes them inflexible, convinced of their own infallibility and unable to change.*" Well put. Humility draws people in, ego pushes them away. Take your pick.

Business owners miss valuable leadership learning moments because their ego is loath to admit they do not know something. Sure, there is a lot you now know you didn't and some topics bore you. But what price are you paying for having mind and ears closed? Since owners are in a command position they feel they are supposed to know everything and if not, risk looking like a moron. *News flash*: all owners are really good at some things, expert even, but lousy at others. It's OK. Just say you don't know if you don't and somebody may pass you a piece of valuable information instead of it never coming due to ego blockages.

I remember how I hated negotiating office leases. There were copious pages and I didn't know what a lot meant and figured it couldn't be in my favor. I mentioned this to a fellow owner who felt the same and said he used a tenant rep. "What's a tenant rep"? , I asked. Someone that did all that and is paid by the lessor. "Seriously? Where do you find one of those?" I asked. Never did another one nor looked for space. Had a tenant rep do it for me. It paid to admit my ignorance.

A good strategy around other owners, all of whom possess knowledge you don't, is to act stupid and continually ask "how so?" or "how did you manage that?" when they mention a successful marketing campaign, their loan went through, they landed a large deal, they restructured, whatever. Remember *Columbo* ? Act like Columbo to obtain helpful information from those who have it! Play to the other guy's ego for a waterfall of useful insights to pour forth. Resist the usual arrogant conversation between two, frequently male, owners consisting of subtle competition of one trying to top the other's numerical data. Stupid.

I was part of an ego deal that cost a competitor $400,000. He asked if I was interested in buying his company because he had trouble. He was in my industry and 15 years older. We talked and an acquisition was something that would add growth. He needed $100,000 down which I obtained and $250,000 was allocated in a non-compete agreement, standard fare because you can't have the seller take the money and return to selling his customers. After eight months it was too much for him not being the boss, much less a younger whipper supervising, even though treated quite well. He quit and went back calling on his customers with the same product working for someone else. I asked him if he was nuts because he was in jeopardy of losing his purchase money. I can't print his response nor did it make sense. Hubris. The judge ruled against him for $400,000. Go figure.

What about the damages from our deadlocked Congress? Egos play in the gridlock and in the Wall Street Debacle. In both, people pay dearly. Don't go there. Decisions made under the influence of ego come undone. Ego mistakes owners make include putting themselves into advertising, going too low just to "win," patronizing people, buying expensive furnishings to impress or leasing office space bigger than you need. I call decision making with too much ego DWI—Deciding While Intoxicated! Investor Warren Buffet is on to its destructive powers. When he sees companies building monuments to themselves he sells the stock.

Ego causes owners to refrain from making painful choices, not from the pain of the choice but the pain of how it reflects on them. Say you need to cut someone, some expense, some perk, something your bottom line needs, but you don't because it " looks bad". Not as bad as it might later from inaction due to a paralyzed ego. Part of being a leader is doing what needs to be done when it needs to be done. Period. You are supposed to be decisive and make the hard choices.

All small businesses look bad some of the time. Maybe most of the time. Don't make this condition worse by making it permanent. Whenever my company has a bad month I tell them and do not hesitate to say "we lost $7,000 this month" which keeps it real. It is just the score of the game and everyone plays best knowing it. Try deploying some humility. It is uncommon but refreshing when a leader is not continually juiced on ego and leaving reality behind. CEO's prefer ego adjectives like "great" and "we are the largest" or "we are the fastest growing," which do not mean much or could mean you are doing stupid things faster than competitors. You are never more authentic that when humble and truthful which is easier than lying.

Moe Lesson

In business, your greatest competitor is yourself, not the guy across town. A big part of beating yourself as a competitor is containing ego. Put the guys across town aside and put that energy into making yourself better. This is hardest for men. We can't help it. It's in our DNA. We want to yell, hoot or honk louder than anyone in the room or on the interstate. Our story must always be more amazing, our numbers always higher. Men must win. No, we won't listen well, ask for directions nor read them. One male complimenting another is a rarity. If it is done it is usually for self-serving reasons rather than true admiration.

To be sure I am on track here I checked with my dog Moe to see if there was a lesson. Moe lives indoors but our other hound, Atticus, lives outdoors. Both are males. When I let Moe out he hikes his leg and does his thing. Atticus immediately goes to the same spot and does likewise. Moe then goes back to the same spot one more time for good measure and to have the last lift. Yes, a real pissing contest between two males accomplishing nothing. So there you go.

There are a few times my "dam the torpedoes, full speed ahead, ninja business warrior, don't-tell–me-what–to-do skills, over-my-dead- body, don't think so" capabilities were needed to repel something threatening my company. But the majority of business battles do not require sending a battleship to a swimming pool.

Be real at all times in leadership efforts. Your followers easily detect it from BS and don't think they don't. Even if you have to say negative things if they are true you still have integrity, a leader's best quality. This lets people be impressed by *you*, way more valuable than depending on amazing stories of your accomplishments. This gets you everywhere as a leader. Humility draws them in—just some even! To be impressive be authentic and real. It is a strong platform for a leader to operate from. Why do you think reality shows are popular? Because people are hungry for real. It should be obvious that operating out of these traits is the most effective for getting followers and building unity. At the moment you are perceived as real is the moment you become powerful.

That said, ego challenged ways of business owners, mostly of men, would do well to counter with the employment of some women. They have their own issues but generally different than males and usually not the destructive ego thing. They mesh easier with men, are more sympathetic to customers and listen better than men. Women tend to be pleasers and men tend to have to be right, even if wrong, and this stuff dissipates valuable company energy so have a good balance. Just sayin'.

When I sold for IBM I enjoyed boasting to my mother of big deals I made and the commission. Instead of getting a proud mother compliment I got a scolding: "Tommy, pride goeth before a fall." Mom did not know a lick about business but did know what got men into trouble. I think a male leader can earn more respect by admitting a failure rather than running from it. A simple "I am sorry, I made the wrong call on that," in front of the employees can, again, draw employees in. Or "our company did not perform in the past three months and I am going to have to make some adjustments so things don't get worse for us. I am very sorry about that."

That Owner Frame Of Mind

At times we are legends in our own minds but other days feel like the mole in the Whack-A-Mole game. During this GR we may feel no more prosperous than an Afghan realtor. A business owner's mind is highly driven, does a lot of good and enjoys distinct periods of happiness and satisfaction not found working for someone. It is an originating point for jobs, careers, innovation and wealth creation.

An entrepreneur is generally admired. But as part of this gig his mind also suffers mental traumas and black holes non-owners don't! Its power switch has only two settings: ON and ON. It must know the future, withstand regular rejection, look at the company checkbook without passing out, and live with the knowledge that 70 per cent fail. We look wistfully at those who bounce, catch, or putt for 10 million. There is Simon wearing a t-shirt while telling people they can't sing making 75 million! How did we get stuck having to earn it!?

When a business owner wakes, providing he slept, his mind is already going. He sprinkles gunpowder on his cereal and begins the day's thought spiral. "Six months into the year and in the red. Dam. This recession is holding back buying. Getting behind on a few payments. The new salesperson seems iffy. Why did I put in the new computer? Why? I guess we lost the Acme deal. Was counting on that. Workman's comp auditor is today. Larry called in sick again. Brother." And that is just the first five minutes of the day. You are more certain than Chicken Little that the sky is falling. You have The Business Owner's Blues.

Too much worry is not a good thing but look at the negative ju ju, and there is plenty of it, the same as quarterbacks do tacklers: "I'll get by them." He feeds off it and that is not for everybody. Even if you are willing you may not be able. Sometimes there are black holes when nothing is working cash flow is negative and all the rest.

One negative thought quickly breeds 379 more. Why does that not work for positive thoughts? One positive thought equals one positive thought. One negative thought breeds exponentially more than that within three seconds. Stuff can get to be too much in business ownership and it is a certainty your limits will be tested. This is part of it.

I learned when experiencing grey to have others help you out of it even though they don't know they are. Find a few close people, employees or otherwise, and be honest with them and that is half the battle right there. Be humble. Listen to suggestions. You will bounce back. Winston Churchill: "When going through hell keep going." Good advice, yes, but a clouded brain can have trouble where to focus to "keep going". In small business the answer would be to focus on sales, more revenue generation. That is where to go, even if you have to fire an admin or tech to afford a sales rep.

Shades of Gray

I have been discouraged enough to quit and sell but things always passed and here I am 32 years later. I chose this route and it has suited me, even if down times are more brutal than I like. With the overall high failure you appreciate the considerable darkness among owners, and that was before the GR. Non-business owners do not realize how good they have it sometimes. If you are a salesperson you either sell or not. A technician either fixes the thing or not. An admin either balances the ledgers or not. Their stuff is a lot of black and white whereas ownership territory is mostly grey and in search of satisfaction.

Protect your owner brain and manage it like any company asset. If having stomach aches, headaches, insomnia, anxiety or depression, take the medicine! I used to be one not wanting to "take anything" but learned I was stupid. Medicines can keep you from getting worse which costs more money. Delegate, exercise, eat right, do not over work, and avoid the negative swirl (think toilet bowl) that can flush positive ideas, and you, if not proactive about stress. The swirl is powerful and easily out duels any positive thought. Positive thoughts, possible money makers, frequently fight for their lives to avoid being flushed. Remember, positive thoughts do not multiply exponentially like negative ones. Protect each one, keep them away from the bowl and never let them circle the drain!

That said, it is good to be King! Or Queen! Nobody can fire you and if an employee displeases, you can decapitate them. Nobody tells you what to do or when. You can take off Mondays. You get market value for yourself, a good thing, right? Some curry favor like American Express, your bank, insurance agent, landlord, and vendors. You can put President on your business card. You even pay yourself your worth! You are a self made business ninja with a castle, even if fire-breathing dragons wait outside to torch you! You conquer all, well most, of what goes against you, and that feels really good. You just have to keep going. You are never there. Persist. Persist. Persist until you just can't, and hopefully that point never comes. I like how my friend and fellow author Jay Myers puts this in the title of his book: *Keep Swinging!*

Owner's Eye

Along with the development of that Owner Frame Of Mind comes The Owner's Eye. Business leaders have their way of looking at things that are different from employees' and most people. You can tell experienced owners by their expression or lack of one. It is similar to a parent's watching kids play happily on the playground but there is no smile on Dad's face. No, he is thinking about possible injuries from falling off the bars, getting into a spat with another whipper or a sudden lightening strike from a looming cloud. When playtime is over THEN dad is glad even though child is sad.

That's how it is through an owner's eye, too, which is usually focused on uncertain future threats, remembering past traumas, and never quite being in the moment. Trifocals anyone? If you feel this you know you are a veteran owner. An owner's eye is never closed. It is not looking at the same page as everyone. It is looking about, taking in the ju ju and processing it through Business Owner 2.0.

Let's see how a well-developed owner's eye should operate and benefit survival. I served in the Navy and they use radar and sonar to look ahead so not to run into anything or smack an iceberg. Owner's eyes employ business radar that looks ahead six months assessing dangers and opportunities. Add a territory? Sell my business? Buy a business? Drop a product? Add a product? Raise prices? Lower prices? Downsize my facility? Fire someone? Stuff like that.

What do you see on your radar? If it is slackers, malcontents, or egomaniacs then boot them! They consume disproportionate shares of business oxygen. If fortunate to see high performers do all to keep them. What if you see a high performing malcontent? Ah, yes, the joys of bossdom. What do you see looking at financial ratios? I know, Armageddon. You can only expect from what you inspect, though, and can never be afraid to look. You will see good stuff too, but the worrisome stuff usually exceeds the good stuff.

The owner's eye should operate like that of a pigeon. Pigeons are great masters of eyeball reconnaissance. They can stroll ground level sidewalks or parking lots looking for certain dangers or food handouts. Once that's done they like to hop to window ledge level and eyeball from just above it all. When they have that in hand they move to the power lines to get the 360 view. Their three views on the world gives them the complete picture which is what you are looking for as well. Develop a similar 3D process for your owner's eye.

The function of an owner's eye is looking around, looking ahead, understanding and interpreting. Looking. Looking. Remember the first word we learned to read? It was *look*! You cannot do so buried in your office selling and fixing things. This makes owner's eyes myopic. Conversely, you become farsighted if aloof from customers and employees. Have your owner's eye look close enough at employees to know their personal problems on some level because they come in the front door and affect the business. Help them if you can, which is good for the employee and the business. This falls into my 'treat everyone differently' philosophy.

I had an ex-employee who liked to say, and I take it as a compliment "Everything is personal with Tom". No HR people please.

Whatever you see you must see it right because margin for error in small business is small. The owner's eye looks at company vital signs like billing, AR, cash flow, employee morale, inventory, profit margins, and sales pipeline regularly. My business produces 700 invoices monthly and I sometimes look at each one. I note billing too high or low and make sure things like mileage are charged if we drove a distance.

I look at inventory for dead stuff and think of uses before it's worthless. I go over payables to know what everyone is charging. This burns company vitals to my brain's hard drive keeping me in command of my numbers (see "the owner must know!"). It helps my brain software stay current and free of viruses. It is estimated a company loses 4% of billing through sloppiness so sweating the details will help get that back too. LOOK!

The Rest Of You

A business leader should take the same Hippocratic Oath as a doctor: first, do no harm! Being a business leader, whatever the company size, is demanding, can take a toll everywhere and compromise life if you are not careful. Business success at the expense of family, faith, health or employees is really failure. We have already spoken of the considerable demands and expectations on you. To not lose family, faith, health or employees be proactively smart about your leadership methods so you do not burn your circuits. Owning a business can quickly become your constant focus and an excuse for not attending to regular living. A bit of this is alright but as a way of life, NO! If it is regular there is something burning down and it could be you. Business ownership should ultimately serve you and not the other way around! No matter how successful you might become business ownership success does not furnish all elements of happiness. Does not.

For some owning a business becomes an addiction. This is not being successful. This will do what all addictions do—destroy something. If you can't manage yourself you will have a hard time managing a company so balance business with outside activities including fitness programs, family activities, hobbies and spiritual. Exercising raises business IQ 20 points. You can't get wealthy without being healthy. Non-business activities cushion stress which lurks around business owners and depletes creativity. You are the company's most valuable asset so protect it like other assets: insure it, maintain it, grow it, and keep it safe. Your energy and stress tolerances have to be above average to hold your role. I say one year of a business owner's life equals one and a half years of a normal person's so owning a business ten years is like working for 15 years (I am only 8 in dog years).

Business owners must bring their "A" game to make it. You have one don't you? This recession has put our minds at Green Beret level. I am ex-military and like military comparisons because business ownership is a form of war. But truly, you need toughness to succeed long term. Not the physical but the mental. Many pass the Green Beret or SEAL physical but far fewer possess the mental stamina that gains elite status. Same for you. You must endure things longer than comfortable to win. Some can. Some can't.

Show employees what you want, demand what you need, set goals and publically praise anyone attaining them. Set performance standards. There is no place for hollow posturing, wasteful moves, shirking, and negativity. No "I cants." Only "here's how I can, boss." It is up to you which attitude you take and accept. It's the difference between success and failure. Employees like results and seeing their leader get them.

It's About Time

Learn to delegate everything except things only you can do which lets you attain full entrepreneurship. Picture yourself as a dealer of time and master of leverage. You, one person, send out directives, orders, suggestions, demands, corrections and goals to be met. Now multiply the number of employees these affect directly, then the customers affected indirectly and you begin to grasp the leveraged effects (good ones, yes?) of your leadership. Assign all tasks an A, B or C level of complexity. Yours is 'A'stuff. These tasks take weeks or months to accomplish. They may be pulling the company out of the red, finding more profitable products, opening a new territory, or taking the company through a product launch. Other 'A' s are maintaining cash flow, managing employees and hiring the right people.

A big 'A' job is the management of capital whether green or human. 'A' tasks are the money makers that create jobs and profitability—or not. These tasks take months or even a year to complete. Your biggest 'A' task is making money or else nothing else matters. The more time focused on that, and the less on non-A the more money you likely make. 'B' stuff takes days and weeks and requires a skill like bookkeeping, IT work, repairing, or proposal writing. Lowly 'C's take only hours and are time vampires to A-people. Most anyone can do them.

Your goal is to spend time on A-tasks and delegate the rest. You won't always be able to but it is your goal. Another way of saying this is that leaders make sure the company keeps the main things the main things. Spending time on 'B's and 'C's makes you a bad dealer of time and less profitable. Pushing away B and C stuff, in turn, makes someone expert at those furthering your goal of becoming the Total A-Man. Mastering this leaves time to be a human. In my years in business I never really worked late, brought home much work, or worked weekends. I did frequently leave early to work out. I was Mr. A and a world class delegator, a big factor in my success and longevity. To further cement these credentials I confess I never filed anything in 30 years. I never had my own file cabinet for anything. Others saw to that.

Care of the 'A' Brain

Put this sign on your desk: "It's About the 'A's! Look at them and try to ignore B and C by delegating them. I have a metaphor on this. I am a motorcyclist and on two wheels you must devote full attention to the handlebars, an A-task, or lack of focus will be hazardous. On two wheels, you go where you look. It is just how it works. If trying to avoid a pothole you look *where you want to go,* not at the pothole, in order for the handlebars to follow the eyes. This is the frame of mind for the owner to navigate danger. It is not hard to spend time staring at business trouble, and that can be B and C stuff too, and we know there is plenty. The way out is to *stare at the solution, to look in the direction you want to go,* and to spend your time and energy there. Don't fixate on the potholes. Delegate the B and C problems so you retain a clear vision of your destination instead of gathering bugs on your teeth.

This A,B C philosophy may fly in the face of the often heard, idiotic management philosophy "I don't ask anyone to do anything I wouldn't do myself." Right. This may be a philosophy but is not sound management philosophy. The only business where it can possibly work is in a solopreneurship where owner and employee are the same person. I do not ask my technician to PM a copier because I would do such myself but because *I do not know how to do it!* I do not ask my bookkeeper to file a 941 and balance the journals because I myself would but because *I do not know how!* Your eventual goal, if you can get there, is to work yourself out of a job and the only way to do that is by delegating and developing employees to do it all regardless of what you would or would not do yourself.

Being a CEO, even if supervising yourself, means getting the most from the least using time management methods that work with you. You can hand write 15 words per minute. You can text, depending upon….well I don't know what, but faster than write. You can type 50 words per minute. You speak 100 words per minute. Video is traditionally said to be worth 1000 words. If you post it on You Tube then that gets multiplied. Email blasts cover ground in a hurry. All point voice mails to employees are good. Meetings where everyone has to physically show are time consuming. Have them towards the end of a day. The point is to find methods that increase management muscle EXPONENTIALLY. The more exponential, the better you leverage time, the better you leverage company expertise, the better the executive. As I like to remind, Steve Jobs, Bill Gates, Fred Smith, Mark Zuckerberg etc. all had the 24 hours you do. Their "exponentiality" (not a real word) is off the charts.

Let's itemize good uses of time that are "A" levers to pull to leverage your efforts in an exponential way:

Hire a person	Fire a person
Change a job description	Design incentive pay
Give formal recognition	Give a talk
Buy a company	Sell a company
Send out direct mail	Hire an ad agency
Adjust prices	Change a vendor
Demand lower prices	Demand what you need
Have a company function	Have an open house
Put on Lunch and Learns	Customer advisory board
Conduct customer survey	Conduct a survey
Make your processes easier	Update technology
Promote someone	Probation for someone
Join network group	Form a Five Group
Set new goals	

Your company moves at the speed you do. At least at the speed you insist upon. As a dealer in time blow the whistle when it expires for a task or when efforts are moving too slowly so employees understand expectations and where the bar is. They move quicker if they know the time limits. Keep a sense of urgency going always which keeps everyone up to speed. You have seen how much better a football team plays in the two-minute drill, right?

As owner of the 'A' brain guard it and design your day in a way you enjoy. Maybe avoid morning traffic. Leave at three and work the rest from a home office. Have staff handle smaller time consumers in your personal life. It is more than OK. This keeps your 'A' brain going longer and everyone is better off. This is why you see big time CEO's and presidents of countries so pampered. It is really to help them stay focused on the monster problems and not let valuable problem solving capability be sucked away. You might say these limo riding execs deal only with A+ stuff. Hopefully that's what they are doing in there.

I love this line from Lori Greiner, a Sharks on Shark Tank, that is poignant: "*Entrepreneurs are the only people willing to work 80 hours a week to avoid working 40 hours a week.*" There is truth in that, and it is telling, but you do not want that to be you. You can't keep that up and it means you are being a bad manager. It also means other things are burning to the ground in your personal life. Support staff should always help prevent this and be saying "I take hassles off my boss—the 'A' brain guy!" proudly helping preserve problem solving brain neurons. Reality for the small business brain may be it has to be more reactive than proactive in leading but small business owners have to be creative to last so leave brain space for it!

This use of time is just vital in determining the longevity of your business shelf life and even your own. I wrote one of my columns on this topic and I reprint it here below:

Approaching Business Burnout
By Tom Pease

Somewhere along the way you take a key fork in the road and it is the wrong one. You decide to burn yourself out.

Many who start into business have the idea of 'building a business' but their management style never lets this happen. Instead, they decide to do everything themselves, decide everything themselves, approve everything, and even wear all this as some sort of badge of honor. It isn't. You might even hear this person proclaim "I work 65 hours a week." Or "I have not taken a vacation in years." Poor you, I say. I would not think much of you as a manager.

The right design for longevity is hiring others that know how to do something too. You even teach them. Then you delegate and get off the Mr. Everything deal. Good decision! Managing is defined as getting things done through others. Doing everything yourself is neither growing a business nor managing one. It is a form of self-employment.

And maybe always being busy doing everything is making you a lousy leader. An invisible one. Maybe one that does not inspire much confidence in others.

I suggest that you spend all that extra time and effort of doing things yourself and put it into recruiting and training a superb employee. The payoff to your business will eventually be bigger. It's how you grow too. Sure it takes more outlay temporarily until the new talent can come on line but that is what you signed up to do. It is part of the business of business.

Hiring solid staff, even if only one person a year, is what will lead you to your business serving you instead of you serving the business. You may not want that right now but you will later.

When I hear an entrepreneur is working all the time I get it. I understand. It can be alright for a time but will not be alright all the time because it will ruin other important stuff in your life.

I have lived a good life for 30 years of ownership in the very tough world of copier sales and have never had anything come easy to me. Nevertheless, I have always been a good delegator. The main reason for that is I had enough to do and was always more than happy to see someone else do it. I actually rarely worked more than 40 hours a week at the office. Of course I think about the business all the time but I can get away from it because I have developed some people.

So, get creative, delegate, hire well, inspire others, and you will grow to tell about it. You wanted to be a long term successful business owner so be one. This is how it is done.

4/25/2010

Don't Use An Office

This is not for everyone but I found it helps me be a better leader. There are more and more examples of it so I may have started it. You have heard of management-by-walking-around. I am coining: management-by-sitting-around. When I got my first real space my office was a former demo room and had no doors. I say doors because the opening was equal to two. I cheerfully moved in. The no door thing proved to be a plus. People walked past and I happily waved. I could over hear the person answering the phone. I kept confidential stuff in the controller's office. People felt they could stop in for a quick chat. All good. "Tom does not have an open door policy", one said. "He has a no door policy.

"It became a trademark and made various statements, all positive. Whenever we moved I specified no doors and the double wide opening. I never liked an office anyway, usually sitting an hour then going on an appointment or preferring to wander chatting up employees and sitting in their offices. As technology advanced, email, cell phone, et al, I could use a screen anywhere and look at my stuff. I conducted hallway meetings, the quickest kind. You are the company's power plant, the enriched uranium, so the closer employees are the more energy they absorb and in turn, are more powerful.

For nuclear energy to percolate compounds must connect and it is so with owner and employees. How much enrichment is there if walled off, door closed, unapproachable, and seen as Moses on a mountain? Not much. I enjoyed my approach, undoubtedly necessary for it to work, but it facilitated instant oversight, quick answers to questions, valuable coaching time, morale building and a general better understanding of what was going on than I would otherwise. All good.

I have leased a lot of space but in the last two moves I specified no office. Why waste the space when the conference room was usually empty so I continue that. While at IBM there was a feature story on the CEO's office. Any CEO of IBM is Moses but he worked at a stand up desk—a sort of podium desk. He had a sit down one, of course, but preferred working at his stand up. There is certainly a trend of businesses using less real estate because we are constantly connected no matter. The web is the new real estate. We no longer need a building for connection, which also makes us less personable, so do even more management-by-sitting-around!

The "P" Laws

There are three important understandings for leaders about human behavior, actual laws of behavior, that make you a better leader. They all start with "P". We take *Parkinson's Law* first. It states that work spreads itself out into the time available to do it. For example, if you have a one person workload that has gone over 100%, maybe into overtime and extra hours and is now 120%, that is not sustainable so you hire another. Now two are doing 120% so each is numerically doing 60%. Not very productive. If you ask them later how it is going you likely get "covered up boss" which is the employees' way of spreading out their work to the available time to do it which is bad news for the boss.

The Peter Principle which states that all rise to incompetence. Of course, not every employee is qualified to be CEO so where does one stop? Where does he begin to permanently get behind on competence? You decide that but everyone hits a ceiling, either voluntary or involuntary, and this applies to owners. The ceiling can be raised with more training. You never know how someone will do in a job until they do the job. If they can do the job then fine, if not, they met the Peter Principle. To limit damage from the Peter Principle require people under promotion consideration to already be doing some work the new job requires and observe that before promoting. When hiring do so on a 90 day probation before making it permanent, requiring a demonstration of competence.

Finally, *The Pareto Principle* states that major consequences are produced by a minority. You know this as "the 80/20 rule" about how 80% of profits come from 20% of customers thus making it vital to know the 20%. This law governs the classic "the plane crashed due to failure of a $10 part." Or, "the production line halted because it ran out of $2 karbonzza clips." Or, maybe you lost a sizable sale because some small thing spooked customer confidence. So make it your business to see that $10 airplane parts never fail, that you never run out of karbonzza clips and that your business inspires confidence always because the small things speak loudly. Another way of stating Pareto is the tail wags the dog. Most leaders try not to let that be the case but we see it happens. My favorite way of stating this principle is THE LITTLE THINGS ARE THE BIG THINGS.

There is another "P" word, not a law, but a quality good leaders need to have. The word is hard to say and even pronounce but it is strongly applicable to leaders. For homework, I want you to look up its meaning. Here it is: you are *perspicacious!*

It is not a P-Law but *Murphy's Law* is well known and must have been written by a former small business owner. It speaks to all leaders: "Nothing is as easy as it looks. Everything takes longer than you expect. If anything can go wrong it will." This could contain the most succinct description of a business owner's life that I should end the book right here. But wait. Something has actually gone wrong with the definition of Murphy's Law. It has become so repeated, so much a part or our lexicon, but researchers now doubt it was Murphy that said it first.

The Military Model

You could do worse than learn from the military model of leadership. Some elements are great to emulate as a business leader. Among them is the focus on mission accomplishment. Of course, you have many missions, just like they do. How does the military go about it? Being a vet I can say first hand it is through thoroughness, preparation, and absolute can-do attitudes that do not leave much room for failure. Taking decisive action is a military officer's forte and here is a story on that. A captain was ordered to take his men across a river and send the enemy into retreat. He went but was not able to get it done. The general asked another captain if he could do it. He said he guaranteed it. He took his men across the bridge and turned around and blew up the bridge, eliminating any chance of retreat. What bridges might you have that need blowing? That prevent you from going all out? From getting it done? That are barriers to accomplishing your mission?

The military uses recognition—medals for valor and combat and marksmanship and so on, to instill pride. The military trains for teamwork and less on individual effort. Ex-military make good salespeople because they are drilled in the results that discipline brings. They make good managers because they understand the power of a team like nobody else. The military model is effective and teaches things not taught in college or off a flip chart and has been effective enough to keep the country free.

A military leadership technique that translates well into business is creating a culture of preparedness. They don't put things off and use time as it is available not when it is convenient. Any group with the mission of accomplishment, of pleasing customers, of making a profit, of being competitive, and of winning, needs a leader who demands such preparedness. Sense of preparedness/urgency is about not letting your group lose focus and feeling there is always a deadline. This produces tremendous achievement.

I watch the Military Channel and was struck by a D-Day story of the Omaha Beach battle. Our guys took a butt whipping with many casualties. All advance officers were killed. There was a single general, general Coda, who remained far back with the attack. He could not believe the carnage but moved himself up to visible leadership of the infantryman who were bone weary and near defeat. Coda rallied them long enough for reinforcements to arrive and the tide to turn. A review of the battle said the greatest American weapon was not armory but Coda's leadership. So often then, leadership can be a decision by a leader to get out front or be brave enough to turn the tide. This does not mean be foolish but there is a fine line between foolishness and bravery.

There may be a tendency for a business owner wanting to be liked and putting that above demanding what is necessary. Big mistake. If you let people slack even 10% you are losing big money. If you have 15 employees, and 10% slack factor, this means you could do without 1.5. Think about what that cost or cost savings means to your bottom line. Military success is about proactive strategy and getting there before the bad stuff. The level of preparedness is high and response to threat is decisive which is how battles are won in business too.

Get there before your competitor, be ready, respond immediately to customers, and solve issues. There you go. It will not happen without the whole company, created by leadership, filled with *willing readiness to deal.* To develop a strong sense of urgency in your company means it is reliably ready to respond anytime. It will be apparent to customers that you have it, or not, and it helps retain them, making you money. It pays for itself. Put up a *Sense of Urgency!* sign.

A final word on leadership. As noted, there are techniques to use and learn and credibility to gain. But leadership is another of those "haves" to have in order to give it. Some of that is just not well defined and is more of an inborn trait that lofts a leader. Certainly a general has something a private doesn't. The president of the United States has something a mayor does not. The CEO of a Fortune 500 company has chemistry a small businessman doesn't.

As a business leader you will spend many hours pouring over the stuff in our next chapter.

Moe's summation: " **We understand leadership concepts well. Dogs are great leaders and helped define the term. We are the first forward at an earthquake, rescue mission, crime scene, SEAL Team Op or as a seeing eye dog. We are the ones leading the humans. We lead by being out front and being brave which is the way it is done.**"

7

Know Your Numbers

There isn't a pilot that does not know how to read instruments. At least a living one. There is not a doctor that can't interpret blood work. Can you imagine an accountant not knowing how to prepare taxes? Yet, there are too many so called business owners that do not know their financial vital signs. They mostly are preoccupied with making deals and doing things they like best, fixing things or selling them, and sometimes ignoring the rest.

This is dangerous and similar to the boiling frog theory which says if you put a frog in boiling water it immediately jumps out and saves its life. If it is put in warm water and the water slowly moved to the boiling point the frog stays in the pot and dies. You could be this frog and suffer a slow death from ignoring your financial data and being lulled to insolvency. Your financial blood work, providing you pay attention to it, gives lead time to identify trouble in time to do something!

This chapter helps you understand the language of business and how to speak it. If you cannot or will not do this then try to get your money back by returning this book because you won't be needing it.

I can think of examples, mostly early on, when I didn't understand important metrics and it cost me plenty. There was when my CPA said I was billing annual contracts and counting the full year's revenue in one month thus way overstating profits when correct is to show one-twelfth each month. Another time I wanted a 35% gross profit margin so took cost times 135% on the calculator thinking this gave it to me. It didn't. That nets a 26% gross margin causing me to make much less than I thought. Still another miscalculation was when I understood to add one year's principle payments on loans to current liabilities, which I hadn't been doing, causing my book value to really drop. These things are critical if not caught. Better yet, understand them ahead of time.

Some may say these were good teaching moments or "ah ha" moments but they were more "uh oh" moments. These examples, and others like them, play out with consequences in our small businesses. Since most owners do not have excess capital it is urgent to know how things are going, or not, adjust, and, *adjust in time* in order to preserve precious capital. Bad news is not nearly as bad as bad adjustments, no adjustments, or adjustments too late to do any good. In fact, it might be said a small business is in one constant state of adjusting! In small business, the longer you wait to remedy the worse it gets.

Here is an example of an eagle eye adjustment from business Jedi Mother Teresa. As head of her order she came to the US for the annual meeting. Fundraising chiefs presented figures of growing donations but also growing expenses that bothered Mother. Right or wrong, she felt it should not take more and more people to collect more and more money but not have much more left over. During a presentation a waiter poured her Perrier water. "How much does this cost?" Mother asked. "Five dollars," he answered. When she got up she thanked everyone for their efforts but said she was cancelling future meetings, that they were too expensive, to mail the documents, and to return the size of the fund raising organization to what it was previously. We could all be more profitable if as vigilant as Mother Teresa.

"You can't manage it if you don't measure it."

Water boils at precisely 212 degrees. It will not boil at 211 degrees. That is the narrow margin between calm and an eruption. Businesses have similar tipping points for which a warning siren is provided by metrics. Quantify everything. Do the math. Measure it so you can manage it. As a business owner you should be a Numbers Nut. Numerical data is your friend because it *provides understanding.* The more understanding you have the smarter you get and the better decisions you make.

Here's how I am with this. I have three dogs and I run my ATV next to each to know their top speed. One runs 30 mph, another is 22 mph and the slowest is 17 mph. I like doing stuff like that but the knowledge helps parcel out their food better. You know not to give the same to the 30 mph woofer as the 18 mph bow wow. A carpenter's golden rule is to measure twice and cut once. Why? Working with such accuracy the carpenter reduces mistakes like lost time and lost lumber. Let me convert this: measure regularly and make more money.

You are familiar with Google and Facebook. They are where they are because they quantify. They quantify mind boggling amounts of data and find smart ways to sell it so look where it got them. They use algorithms measuring the world but all you need are accurate financial statements and then you have the data to do smart things too. You cannot run your business lacking understanding. Why would you do that?

Some say they "are not good with numbers." Get in another line of work. Business is about the numbers. They are all based on simple grade school arithmetic, so, providing you graduated eighth grade you can be a business math genius. Keeping a good eye on the numbers helps you make timely informed adjustments so you can keep doing what you like doing. That should be reason enough. If you are a numerical slob you risk losing what you like doing.

You Are A Businessperson!

Certainly you signed up for entrepreneurship to satisfy your passion and pursue your craft. But since it is a business, you have to pursue numerical metrics just as passionately. You may not be doing this and if not, it is inexcusable and deadly. You don't have to prepare them but must know what those numbers mean *because you are a business person!* Businesses graze on greenbacks 24/7 like cows do grass. Sometimes the field is green and sometimes brown. The cow knows the difference and adjusts and doesn't wait. You may have a green pasture, a brown one, a weed filled one, a diseased one, an overgrazed one, an unfertilized one, or even a barren one. You can't tell what is causing the problems without soil readings that show the problem. The same goes in identifying problem business conditions diagnosed by analyzing the numbers. You need the tests and analytics that show what shape your business is in. Most come off your financial statements.

Again, all business numbers are just arithmetic—addition, subtraction, multiplying, dividing, percentages and ratios. That's it, so this stuff is easily within your grasp. We are not talking algebra, calculus or algorithms. The important thing in business accounting is the interpretation of the numbers. Are they trending up or down, increasing or decreasing, and what does this mean? What are the target numbers that indicate a healthy condition? An unhealthy condition? Or, a let's get the heck out of here condition? How am I in relation to industry benchmarks? That is the important stuff for a CEO. Lucky for you, all these numbers, ratios and formulas are in this chapter. Tear out these pages and carry them until you have these terms down. Then ask your accountant or banker to quiz you on them and they will be impressed. For further clarification Google any of them.

Financial Statements

Financial statements are the great common denominator among all businesses. Whether you are Wild Cat Oil Drillers, Inc., IBM, or Delta Groove Yoga Company, all have the same components in their statements. Financial statements provide the ultimate financial picture of your business. This term means two different compilations—the income statement and balance sheet both prepared by a bookkeeper for whom you have affectionate nicknames such as The Grim Reaper. It is fine if you do not know how to prepare the statements. I don't.

Hopefully you are not one of those business owners who thinks the CFO of his company is its CPA or accountant. You are always the CFO, even if you employ a CFO. It is your numerical universe to master, or not.

Bookkeepers and accountants look through microscopes to do what they do while owners use telescopes to stay on the big picture. The number crunchers read the tea leaves but remember they do not know how to make tea. That is your job. Accountants are historians. They do an excellent job of telling you what has happened and how things are. They cannot measure your future which is where you and your telescope come in. It is up to you to read those statements and know why something happened, good or bad, and what is going to happen, good or bad. That is what you signed up for.

In accounting everything has to balance to the penny. To the penny? Yes, that is the fail safe of accounting and the DNA of financial statements. When I was first told that early in my career by my bookkeeper my response was "That's impossible, isn't it?" This aroused her deep concern. It is not impossible and it is what bookkeepers do, thank goodness. Accounting is an exact discipline and the way to exactness is keeping 'balance'. You hear this word from accountants. "I am out of balance 18 cents!" Oh, the horror. I used to reach in my pocket and offer it but that just showed I was an accounting idiot. That 18 cents means something is wrong somewhere and, even though only by 18 cents it can mean a larger number went wrong somewhere.

At the heart of keeping balance are debits and credits. Debits must equal credits. When they do things balance and the bookkeeper has it right. Example: A widget in inventory costs $1000. It shows as a current asset on the balance sheet under 'inventory'. Somebody buys it. Cash is debited $1000 and inventory credited $1000. They cancel each other, so to speak, and things stay balanced. Say you receive $500 in parts from a vendor who you now owe $500. Inventory is credited $500 and accounts receivable debited $500. Get it? So the *balance sheet* has two sides—the asset side which totals good stuff like cash, inventory, accounts receivable, paid in capital, and depreciating assets and the liability side which totals the 'bad' which is what you owe. The difference between the good stuff and the bad is book value. Hopefully it is a positive.

The balance sheet and income statement are snapshots of your business at the end of month or fiscal year. Keep a running twelve months and refer to them often. They are fluid and as you read one it is already out of date. Financial statements are compiled and read the same no matter if a 5 person company or 50,000. The numbers are just bigger. Once fluent in interpreting yours impress friends as you analyze General Motor's pointing out areas of concern. "I see their current ratio is a bit less than ideal." Just need a calculator.

The *income statement* is entirely different from the balance sheet and also called 'profit and loss' or P&L. It compiles sales for the month, the 'top line', subtracts cost of goods sold and labor to produce those sales and arrives at gross profit. From the GP is subtracted all expenses such as rent, gas, utilities and payroll including yours. Hopefully, totaled expenses are smaller than GP and you made money. If not, you lost. Small businesses do not make a profit every month. They must make one yearly though and that is after owner pay.

I explain a typical year for my business as five months of making a little and five months losing a little. One month of the year we make really good money. One month we lose bad money. The difference between the really bad month and the one really good month is profit for the year, which is never very much! Ride the roller coaster. My VP says my tombstone will read: "He Broke Even."

Financial statements are compiled monthly the day after month end. Most accounting software automatically spits them out if data has been entered correctly through the month which it probably hasn't been. The bookkeeper usually has to investigate, tweak and tune. That is a primer on financial statements, the mother of all financial data and your financial GPS.

**CAUTION. You Are Entering the
"*BECOME A BUSINESS PERSON*" Zone!**

The following sections have considerable arithmetic and formulas. Proof readers have said it is dry and sometimes tedious reading. I agree. I have tried to present it as simple as possible but it is what it is and it is important! Follow along with a pencil, pad and calculator to get the most out of it. Take a break or two and maybe put on an oxygen mask.

Following A Dollar

This exercise helps understand financial statements better and forms your accounting brain. Start with something in inventory and bill it to your customer for $1 sale. Let's follow its impact on the statements, first the P&L. You relieve inventory of the cost of the item, say, 50 cents. You have a receivable for $1. The $1 goes into your top line as revenue. The 50 cents is entered into 'cost of goods sold' and the net gain of 50 cents is now part of gross profit on the P&L. When the customer pays his $1 invoice show $1 into cash and remove $1 from AR since it is now collected.

As sales dollars wind through your financial statements the same dollars receive different interpretations about their significance. If five people view the sale there will be five different observations depending upon who you are. I see a $10,000 sale and happily say "OK, good sale there. We made a decent margin." When the controller sees it: " That is ABC Company and they take 90 days to pay. It will be a while before we see that money." The banker chimes in with "AR over 60 days does not qualify as collateral on your borrowing base." The sales rep says "It's not fair I have to wait so long for my commission." The service manager complains "Why did we not get a service contract with that sale?" And so it goes.

Working Capital

Working capital is the difference between current assets and current liabilities on the financials. This is the money available to circulate your company's veins to pay bills, buy inventory, and make payroll. It is not the checkbook balance. It is among the most important numbers. If placed on a dashboard it's the speedometer. Ideal working capital is expressed two ways. One is as the *current ratio* which is current assets divided by current liabilities. This ratio must be at least 1:1, the barest acceptable to be able to pay your bills, up to about 1.75:1 to be fluid. Below 1:1 means you have negative working capital, meaning no working capital, and life is miserable.

The other way, which gives the dollar amount, is the difference between current assets and current liabilities plus one year's principle payments on loans. It is critical to put 12 months total principle payments into current liabilities because they do not show up anywhere else including the P&L. Early in my still-learning-to-be-a-real-businessperson years, my bookkeeper gave me nice financial statements. It showed profit and I was proud and showed them to my banker with who I had a term loan.

He said two important things: "I don't see any entry on your P&L for allowance for income taxes nor your twelve month principle payments totaled in current liabilities." Say what Mr. Pinstripes? Any interest expense in loans is entered on the P&L but principle payments are not. So Mr. Banker says "You are showing $25,000 in profits but have $30,000 in principle payments so you are going backwards cash-wise thus we will not be able to loan." I immediately made a few adjustments! So keep track of principle payments. Treat them like an expense mentally even though they are not treated so from an accounting standpoint.

To find your company's ideal working capital add up one month's expenses, one month's debt service, one month's cost of goods sold, plus AR total. When working capital is low the business is said to be undercapitalized. Then again, most bankers say the term 'small business undercapitalization' is redundant. There are things that increase working capital (good) and things that decrease it (bad).

Increases Working Capital	Decreases Working Capital
Making a profit	Losing money
Borrowing money	High principle payments
Selling fixed assets	Bad debt
	Paying income tax

It is hard to increase working capital without selling products that throw off more than just a monthly fee. You need to sell hardware too, with margins in the 30% range, combined with annual inventory turns of about 6, plus annual agreements paid up front, to build cash without borrowing. You can see by this example the bearing one number has on another and why you need to know their interpretations.

We're Making Money But Have No Money!

Most business owners spend considerable time chasing money. Attaining positive cash flow is the Holy Grail of small business. In all that you generate operating a business the highest priority is *generating cash*. Repeat to yourself frequently: "Cash on hand. Cash on hand. I must design my finances to always have some cash on hand! "

A business with chronic poor cash flow is one with the equivalent of business heart disease. There will be blockages and maybe a heart attack. But you can prevent such and take measures to reverse it. Positive cash flow is not a term or number used on the balance sheet or income statement. It is simply the amount coming into a business, say, in a week, and the amount going out during the same week after paying current expenses. If more came in than went out that is positive cash flow. You might be positive for a week or negative over a month but it must be positive over a year. Cash flow has a lot of bearing on your checkbook balance or lack of one.

One of the root causes of poor cash flow is a business that begins under- capitalized. Don't start that way and do yourself a big favor. You can be adequately capitalized from the start if it is just you. Surely you can adequately capitalize one person or you shouldn't start the business. Once you have, and make enough profit to pay yourself a living wage, then add another person and repeat. This builds a more solid cash flow machine rather than always over reaching your cash. If you are already up maybe you need to cut back a bit to live within your cash.

Negative cash flow does not necessarily change total working capital. Negative flow can mean you are losing money, yes, or more frequently, have too much capital in illiquid inventory or uncollected AR. For example, you eat daily and visit Kroger weekly which suits household cash flow. If you bought six month's groceries at one time it would not change the outlay you normally make for six month's groceries but would have a negative impact on family cash flow for six months. It might mean no cash for gas, utilities, rent and thus life comes to a screeching halt. Same for a business. The owner has a juggling act to balance the outs with the ins. Usually an owner knows how much cash has to go out he is just not sure how much is going to come in.

I remember my first encounter with the cash flow bogey man. I was minority owner, the sales guy and bringing in the money. I asked the partner who did the accounting how much we had in the bank. He replied "Right now? None." I thought it meant we were broke but it meant customers had not paid. We were in a period of 'cash no' instead of cash flow. This goes on all the time in small business. It just cannot go on for a long time. It's like the one about the banker asking his customer to "Tell me about your positive cash flow, to which the business owner replied "I am positive I have no cash flow."

To generate positive cash flow requires a business model to do this. You have crucial business design choices that determine cash flow. Here is one: sell more! You can, for example, decide to open a restaurant and sell food one plate at a time and may obtain a measure of success. You could also cater which sells meals 100 at a time. If successful at each, which do you think generates the most flow? The caterer, of course. Do both.

It does not take much more effort to go after the bigger cash cow than the smaller piggy bank. My sales manager says : "it's about squirrels, zebras and elephants. Bagging a squirrel feeds you for a day, a zebra a week and an elephant for six months." Yeah. So make sure you elephant hunt and know how to bag one if you get the chance. Go after bigger cash cows some because they provide the largest profit in the shortest time. At least have some in your business plan. Selling products characterized by healthy margins, is how small businesses grow and scale. It is much harder one low margin plate at a time.

Here are things that increase flow and get more dough quicker. Other than robbing a bank, try these:

- Change invoice terms to 'net 10 days' or even 'due upon receipt'. I like 'net now'. Kidding.
- Bill daily. Do not stockpile billing. The faster it goes out, the faster it comes in. Bill in advance if you can.
- Sell inventory quicker. Get rid of dead inventory for some amount. EBay it. Maybe rent it
- Delay payables as long as you can get away with. Then pay them with a credit card which gives you 30 more days. Some states take credit cards to pay sales taxes.
- Barter. Pay bills the old fashioned way and work them off with the goods and services of your business. That's where the term 'trade' originated!
- Get a bank loan. Borrow money.
- Make more profit. Eliminate unprofitable things. Cover all expenses when charging a customer.
- Sell assets. These would be long term assets such as furniture, equipment or fixtures. Or sell them to a lease company and then lease them back to have your cake and eat it.
- Factor. This is selling AR to an entity called a factor. Banks have factor depts. as do finance companies. This is not a loan and it does not depend on your credit rating but the credit of your customer. Factors buy AR for cash taking a cut.
- Collect AR better. Hire someone to do this if only part time. Consult an attorney for anything over 90 days.
- Ask customer to prepay for an order in return for a discount.

- Take a penalty and pay payroll taxes and sales taxes one month late.
- Renegotiate loans, leases or rentals to more favorable terms.

Lack of positive cash flow, if constant, drains business oxygen. It hurts morale and increases stress on the owner and the business. It can force an owner to make bad decisions and pass up profit opportunities. It is universally described as the number one problem of small businesses so treat every dollar like it was one hundred dollars. When one is low on cash he is said to be cash poor. You are in good company. There are plenty of millionaires that are cash poor. They have a net worth on paper of over a million dollars, usually due to illiquid assets, yet may have trouble coming up with much cash.

Business owners can be overly optimistic and have plans that never get going because they do not generate up front cash fast enough. Remember the line from *Jerry McGuire* that Cindy, my VP, repeats whenever she sees my new ideas brewing and what I think I could do … and I am feeling it … and I am believing I am onto something that … and I am excited about something new … and I know so and so did this successfully in another city … and I think we could … and she breaks in and messes it up with SHOW ME THE MONEY!! Oh, yeah. That. These times closely resemble the brain surge of start-up mode. It is always good to have someone helping maintain your business sobriety. If you don't at least remember this: cash on hand tells you what you can do today and profit what you can do tomorrow. To contemplate any new sort of expansion you need to be in a profitable position first.

Accounts Receivable

Collecting accounts receivable is critical to attaining positive flow, that is, if you extend credit. If a cash only business that is a very good thing and AR isn't an issue. That means you have cash cows which are inventory that turns quickly for cash and good margins. Examples are women's cosmetics, lottery tickets, Harley Davidsons, iPhones and a cup of Starbucks. I never had a cow or even a calf. Accounts receivable are like humans because they age, turn delinquent, get written off and go to court. AR is parasitic to positive flow and business's well being. Then again, if you do not offer terms you lose business. When you sell on credit all you have is an IOU which is Wimpy saying he will gladly pay you Monday for a hamburger today. You have delivered your goods or services so the customer is now in your debt, hopefully not long.

Costs for collecting AR is the classic intersection where profit verses cash flow meet. I remember when I first arrived here. My AR was piling and the aging columns moving from 30 to 60 to 90 (accounts deceivable?) with rapidity and we never had cash stay in the check book. These invoices were service and supplies in the $200-$300 range. To get it in I asked the office manager to make calls but she had other stuff to do too. I sometimes had my wife call but she hated it. What to do? Hire somebody. I did not like paying $30,000 a year to chase money owed me was my reasoning. Any senior business owner hearing a younger one say this is chuckling. What you are doing is making money but have no money. Hiring a person to herd AR turns this around: "I am not making any money but I have money!" Ah yes, the mind ninja-ing of a business owner.

Once AR is booked it shows as income and contributes to profit. An AR person's salary decreases profit but if you never collect the AR, or it takes forever to do so, it was never going to do you the good you had in mind as you stared at it. Once I hired an AR person cash flow increased more than I was paying. She signed up a collections attorney that took harder stuff like 90 days (accounts deceivable?) for a 25% cut and helped get that in too. These are the problem people you turn over to collection specialists. A collection attorney gets results and preserves sanity. Sometimes they collect just by writing a scary letter.

Price It Right

Price it right does not mean price it low. It does not mean price it "fair" either. There is no such thing as a fair price. The only price you want is one that supports your business and one customers pay. There is not a more crucial element to small business success, no more important strategy, than pricing things so they support life. Setting prices is not an exact science and has some art to it. It has a discipline element to it. It has an accounting element to it. It has a competition element to it. It has a timing element to it. Got all that? Too often the answer is no. I firmly believe you get the price you feel you should. It is critical that what you feel you should get is based on what you need to get.

Fix firmly in your mind what it takes for your business to be profitable and let that form your pricing. Here is one pricing point that is certain: your plan, as a small business, cannot be becoming the low price leader. It will not get you there. Low price warfare is for the big boys, won by them and the Internet. It requires hundreds of millions of sales revenue which you cannot attain. Most of that is hard goods, of course. Think Amazon, Best Buy, Wal Mart, Home Depot, eBay, etc. But these behemoths have weaknesses that leave lucrative areas to you, service work being one of them. Service work, based upon skilled labor, does not get scaled out of the small business market like hard goods. Offer service on the really hard stuff to fix, whatever that may be, in your industry, stuff not everyone works on nor has a walking around knowledge of because *where there is mystery there is margin.*

Most business owners are price intimidated and will, in a nanosecond, because they will not be beat, go lower than some idiot's low, low price and both engage in a sort of race to the bottom. When I began my business I ran into competitors like this and it made me question myself. I was noticeably higher but with a price that allowed for sales commission and profit. Some competitors left scant for either. I asked my manufacturer if he sold the machines cheaper to other dealers. He said no. I said "I don't get it, what are they doing selling so low"? I asked. " Good question. I have seen this. They are going out of business by design." And they were gone within a year because they were caught up with winning and little else.

I saw so much of that that I chose it as the title of my first book. The rules for staying in business are the same for everyone and one of those is pricing allows for profit. It is not uncommon for two competitors to get into a price battle. Usually it is ego related. The smart guy is the one who pulls out of this nonsense first and returns to sound financial principles. This may mean you have to become a bit smaller, drop in a ranking in your city or with your manufacturer, and lose a few bragging rights. WHO CARES!? Stay in business.

Another pricing folly is falling for the Greater Fool Theory. Say you are in a deal and the customer says (truthfully?) your competitor recommended Model 6 with an a, b, and c for $3,000. Not to be outdone, you say "I can do a Model 6 with an a, b, c, *and* d for $2,800." If the competitor's recommendation is not right, say it is foolish, and you assume it is right and try to out quote it, you become The Greater Fool. Start from square one and do not take the lazy route of accepting a competitor's recommendation. Best to go with prices and recommendations that work for you no matter what someone else does. Don't bite! Some deals you walk from. If they had little profit you didn't really lose much. The good news is all competitors are not idiots and want to earn business and make money. Weak low ballers cause headaches for a while but not a long while. Maintain your margins if you want to be around. That is a skill to be learned and a frame of mind to keep.

So what should you charge? Some guidelines. If you go to the customer charge $100 an hour, plus mileage if driving 20+ miles. If customers come to you then $75 an hour. With hard goods average 35% gross margin. This means some deals are lower and some higher. Small items, like bolts, brackets, and hardware need even 75% gross margin because of their small dollar. If you sold toothpicks you may need a 500% margin! Conversely, if selling expensive products, say vehicles, the margin may be 20%. The point is at month end you need a critical mass of profit to float and the right pricing is essential. If your products quit bringing decent margins find newer products instead of accepting lower prices.

Another pricing method is 'price it backwards'. Take average monthly revenue and, if short of profitable, go through all invoices and tinker with prices. "I could raise this labor rate a bit, increase charge out cost to sales reps, charge for mileage or delivery, require a minimum purchase, sell by the case only," and the like, until into the black.

Asking entrepreneurs how they price can be humorous. "It seemed about right. It is what my Uncle Harry said to charge and he owns a business. We try to set a fair price. It depends if it is the end of the month or not. We go a little under a competitor. We always give a discount. We do what it takes to win. I had prices figured but Dad said they seemed high. I watch The Price is Right." Might as well channel the Price Fairy. Varying prices all over, and setting them unprofessionally, is like taking more or less blood pressure medicine based upon how you feel that day.

It is the steady discipline, that word again, of a prescribed regime that wins the day and pricing is like that. It should not depend upon what the business conditions or frame of mind is this week. I learned a valuable lesson on pricing from IBM. They gave the price and that was that. IBM did not discount or give free stuff. They did sell the best, had the best, and customers gladly paid. I hear you, we are not IBM! The lessons are still there, though, and just as valid for a small business. Since price was never a variable as an IBM sales person two very good things happened 1) You learned to sell on merit and benefit, the best way, and 2) You accepted the price believing it to be worth it and that belief helped get the price.

When I set a price, especially with a new product, I first sell the salespeople and myself that it is right. Never let a salesperson set a price although invite their feedback. Salespeople usually think a price is made better by being made lower never mind the effect on the business. There is nothing more devastating to sales confidence in a product if the owner has a price range as variable as Larry King's love life. Discount 15% and that is it. This alone retains value in your product which returns more value to your business. If this price is not working then adjust it but if enough deals are accepted then stick. Salespeople want lower prices because it makes their job easier. Price selling is lazy selling and not selling for that matter.

Making a profit is not a painless process but a necessary one so be willing to walk from stupid deals to maintain price integrity. Walking from low ball deals, and showing sales personnel the line, nets more profit in the long run than trying to get every skinny sale. Not maintaining price integrity lets loose price cancer which eats margins and salespeople. Have a talk with yourself that includes this guidance: "You do not want all the business, only the profitable kind." It is fine and advisable to sell down to actual cost to dump product not selling. Maybe move it on eBay or Craigslist and not affect local marketing efforts. Stale inventory saps working capital and its mere presence makes it harder to focus on money making newer stuff. Try not to pay much commission on these sales.

Methods and Formulas

I start this topic with the simplest pricing formula and terminology even veterans get wrong: *the difference between gross profit margin and mark up.* Here it is—if you buy something for $50 and sell it for $100, this is what happened: gross profit is 50%.and markup is 100%. *Mark up and gross profit are two different things.*

Here is a similar goober. An owner decides on a 25% profit margin. He pays $100 and then hits 125% on the calculator giving a selling price of $125. This does not net a profit of 25%. It nets a 20% profit because $25 profit divided by the selling price of $125 gives you the 20%. To set the selling price that has 25% profit take the cost of the item ($100) divided by the inverse (.75) of the profit target (.25) which gives you the selling price of $133 (100 divided by .75). If you want a 40% gross profit in a selling price of something you paid $100 for divide the $100 by .60 (inverse of the 40%) for a selling price of $250. Can you just imagine the amount of damage thinking you were getting a 25% profit margin but weren't?

Businesses speak in percentages because they are easily understood. You may want a 10% price increase or 12% decrease or a 5% interest rate. A very key business metric is *percentage of increase* and *percentage of decrease.* I'll give their formulas after illustrating how useful they are. My salesperson was upgrading a machine and the new one was 21 pages per minute while the old one 17, four pages per minute faster. This did not seem like much difference to the customer and left them unimpressed. The wise salesperson then rephrased saying "this is a 23% increase over your previous speed." The customer changed his tune admitting it was more impressive than it sounded, exactly the effect of speaking in percentages. To figure percentage of increase take the difference, using above example, between the two, which is 4, and divide that by the original machine speed of 17. Next, compute 4 divided by 17 which reads .23 which means 23% increase.

For the percentage of decrease take the difference between the two numbers, say one is 18 and dropped to 13, and divide that number, which is 5, by the original number which was 18, and you get .27, a 27% decrease.

Itemizing

This is a discipline for obtaining best prices. Think like restaurants and how they present their menus. They call it ala cart. There is usually a separate charge for every item. Owners can get sloppy and throw out one price for everything. I get the simplicity and nothing wrong with it per se if you *first itemize* everything on a separate worksheet that lists all costs. This is where pricing deficiencies show up-owners just do not realize true costs. Once true cost stares back at you, in black and white on paper, it brands into your brain true cost and *forces* you to deal with reality. This, in turn, facilitates smarter pricing thus making more money and staying in business. Let's take a look.

Cost of goods	$1.00
Freight in	.06
Labor Burden rate	.20
Sales commission	.20
Taxes	.02
TOTAL	$1.48

So now you have all costs and want a 30% margin in the selling price. Divide cost by the inverse of your desired gross profit margin, 30% (.30), inverse being .70. Divide 1.48 by .70 for a selling price of $2.11 to support life. There are some pricing discipline gurus who say the first thing to add to cost of goods (COG), when arriving at selling price, is the profit.

Some prefer one all-inclusive price while others want it broken out or itemized. This can help buyer and seller see areas of legitimate charges but can also open arguments about them-clear as mud, I know. It is up to your sharp-as-a-samurai mind to decide what to do when. But you see this plenty. Bought tires lately? Tire: $120. Balancing: $5. Valve stem: $3. Disposal fee: $4. Road hazard warranty: $3. And so on. How about a hospital bill: Room: $205 . Bandages: $66 … bed pans: $45 … do you really want me to take this one on because I will soon get into swabs, medicines, wheelchair use, meals… and run out of pages.

Credit card statements, phone bills, bank statements etc., all have itemized charges and fees that, for the most part, have actual basis. It goes on a lot and from the biggest companies. Do take all your items and charge for them *somehow*. As a business person try, I repeat try, to stop using the word free or no charge, as appealing as it is. It is not likely anyone is giving your business much free stuff. Using this word too much may cost plenty over time and make you a lazy seller. Making a profit is not a painless process. You must work at it and pricing is one of those areas.

I remember a financial seminar early in my career. At its end the presenter said he had a tip that would pay for our trip and all future ones. He asked if we used rags, oils, screws, clips and swabs in our service calls, and everyone agreed. These were too small to itemize and nobody in the class was. " Add $4.95 to each billable call for MPS which stands for miscellaneous parts and supplies." I did and do so to this day. It is a legitimate cost but one you wouldn't think much about. When I opened Kawasaki I told the service department to put this charge on all tickets. I can only imagine the total of these $4.95's in my 30 years. Something to think about.

It is important to raise prices annually. Most companies do, big and small but they might be on hold during this GR. It is, none the less, something you should do if prices to you are being raised. GR or not, it has not stopped medical premiums, gasoline, food, eyeglasses, airline tickets, data plans and other stuff from rising. Your price increases are usually small to any one customer, around 5%, to cover inflation and cost of living, but are important to profitability. If you respond to these increases by increasing your prices, it will likely not drive away customers although it may cost a few. Increasing costs are any business owners' challenge and must be neutralized. To ignore them is not dealing with them.

Every dollar of cost increase is another off your bottom line so not something you responsibly ignore. It can be more beneficial to lose a few customers to get the overall increase. Either that or have a big enough sales increase whose profits cover it. Some owners go years not raising prices which may put them 15% behind the eight ball, having to sell 15% more to stay even, after inflation. You can't afford that. Customers may balk at paying any increase and you may balk at the same. Speaking of such, you can probably get any price lowered today by balking, yelling and getting angry. It is a tactic you may have both used and experienced. And so it goes.

Ratios Are The Businesses' Dashboard

When driving a business it is your hand on the wheel and feet on the pedals. If your mission control feeds accurate information to those hands and feet you make the right moves and don't crash. Financial ratios are gauges that feed that information to you on how things are with the business's engine. As you fly your business, instrument flight rating required, you need eyes on these gauges to keep you focused. These ratios are comparison numbers and are simple to compute.

They give you the direction of the business by telling you if things are increasing, decreasing or trending. There are four categories: efficiency ratios, liquidity, leverage and profitability ratios. These will be the handful you need. We covered the *current ratio,* the most important liquidity ratio. Here are others. The "/" symbol means "divided by" in ratio world. The result is a decimal point followed by two numbers such as .03, which means 3% or .11 which is 11 percent.

Quick Ratio: Current assets-inventory/current liabilities. Another liquidity ratio, sometimes called acid test, that checks what working capital is without including inventory. Goal is 1:1.

Return On Assets (ROA): Net income/Avg. Total Assets. This is a profitability ratio. Try to be in double figures.

Return On Equity (ROE): Net income/equity. This is the annual return percent on the capital invested. Look for double figures.

Profit Margin: Net income/sales. The bottom line as a percentage of the top line.

Inventory Turns: Cost of goods sold/Avg. inventory. This is how many times a year you completely sell out of your inventory. Want this number to be 6+.

Debt to equity: Total liabilities/book value. Want this number to be four or lower. Tells what part of the company you own vs. creditors.

Return on investment: net profit/total investment. This one tells you how profitable your investment is. Shoot for double figures. The total investment here means the total invested as applies to total money committed to do something.

Average collection period: 365/yearly sales revenue/avg. AR. Any owner must know this number if you extend credit. It tells you how fast you actually collect. Your goal might be 30 days. Compare the number with the collection terms you state on your invoices.

Gross Profit per Employee: shoot for $13,000 per month for all non administrative employees.

Burden Rate: number of actual work hours / the total cost of the employee including benefits. Say total cost is $50,000 a year divided by 1,794 yearly work hours equals $27.80 cost per production hour.

Hurdle Rate: This is the minimum acceptable return on a project a company may invest in. The higher the risk of the investment the higher hurdle rate it will be assigned. A low rate may be 10% and a high rate 50%.

Ratios are also used to benchmark a business. A benchmark is the optimum number in any measurement category for the industry classification of that business. They are goals and attaining them increases chances of staying in business. Each industry has different numbers for its benchmarks such as optimum revenue per square foot if a retail business or gross profit per employee for any business. For example, an Apple store averages $5000 in annual sales per square foot.

Benchmarks tell the owner where the limits are. For example, if you own a restaurant you need to know how many waiters it takes to serve 200 customers. It can be hard to know going by the seat of your pants or asking the wait staff. You can't go by that because you could be easily mislead, to the detriment of your business, but the restaurant industry knows so go by that. A pilot needs to know the take off speed and stall speed for the plane. He certainly wouldn't ask the flight attendant what he thinks. The owner must know! Find your benchmarks from bankers, trade associations or Googling. Accountants are sources for ratio info and can check yours for correctness. There are tweaks between businesses types, for example those cash only and those that extend credit

Gross Profit Is King.

More important than revenue or ratios is *gross profit*. Gross profit is king. Gross profit is king. Gross profit is king. You can tell when I am obsessed because I repeat it three times. The important part of sales proceeds is the part you keep, the GP. It is what you work for and the important number. If sales are up, but GP down, you cannot say business is "up". It is, in fact down. If revenue was down, but GP up, business is up. Gross profit, not to be confused with net profit, is total sales minus the cost of goods sold, COGS. COGS is the actual cost of hardware sold plus the actual salary of technicians that produced billable labor. All other expenses are paid out of GP and not figured into COGS.

Total revenue just does not tell much about a business like GP does. If a business sells $20,000 with a GP of $5,000 it helps itself the same as a one selling $10,000 and netting the same $5,000. A business operating on a 20% gross margin must sell twice one with a 40% margin. Both net the same GP. Of course, if the GP goes too high you lose sales and GP that came with them. Think of it like this. There are two men each growing to six feet in height. One weighs 300 pounds and the other 150 pounds. Big difference! But both are the same height.

The point is revenue is relevant but the GP is more relevant. For example, you hear real estate companies claim a billion in sales but the homes are not their inventory and the real estate company gets half the 6% commission which is its real revenue. In my sales department we do not even count revenue. We count the gross profit and base commission on it. Small businesses need higher GP percentages than bigger companies because they cannot attain their economies of scale. Pay big attention to gross profit and less to revenue although both hopefully grow in tandem.

It's a Write Off!

This is a phrase to be heard mostly from non-business savvy people trying to sound like they are but in the process show they aren't. A write off is another phrase for tax deduction. That is all it is. It is not free money from the government but it is a "discount" on your income tax bill. If you spend $1000 on rent or $100 on a coffee service both are allowable business expenses thus tax deductions reducing your tax liability. So if you are in the 25% income tax bracket the rent expense reduces your tax liability by $250 and the coffee service does the same by $25. Sometimes people fib on their business expenses to increase their deductions but that would not be our subject here. A write off is a good thing but you would not go around spending as many $1000 things to save $250. It still costs you $750 remember.

A tax deduction should not be confused with a tax credit. A tax credit is a wonderful thing but there are not many out there at this time that I am aware of. A tax credit is an amount allowed by the IRS that lets you take 100% of it off your tax bill once that is figured. So if you owe $2,000 after all deductions and somehow qualify for a tax credit of $1000 you get to take 100% of that off your tax due. Tax credits are issued by the government from time to time to reward some business effort with a high degree of difficulty or risk such as trying to make lighting bugs into a renewable energy source.

Employee Numberheads

A power move is turning employees into Numbers Nuts and this is a beautiful thing. I stress that no matter an employee's job part of it is learning to be a businessperson which means knowing the numbers. My employees can price for the right margin, can compute the percentage of increase or decrease, know our working capital limits, an ugly price or cost from an acceptable one, and how much we made or lost. From this education comes beautiful moments like: "Bossman, this group of Bing Bang Widgets is piling up and not moving. Our cost is $10,000 which eats 5% of our working capital so I recommend we wholesale it to get our capital back."

When you school them in the numbers they feel pride of ownership and even smugness. They are in the know. They are businesspeople! I also do not tolerate them speaking in un-quantitive terms like "a lot, a little, a bunch, a good bit, it's high, or not much." I tell them these terms are not helpful and not business terminology and to substitute the actual number instead. That way we are both smarter and quicker about the situation.

I once had a month we lost $28,000 in my 21 employee 2.5 million dollar company. I thought I would become catatonic within the next five minutes. I was horrified and did not think such a number was possible. I let fly the expletives and called a meeting to distribute this financial to everyone to share the misery. Of course, such a thing has pluses and minuses but I was in search for *anything* positive.

My folks are number savvy but still came the comments. "Wow, why do we pay so much rent? Should we still sponsor our softball team? How come we have a membership to the fitness club? (Oh, boss trying to stay healthy so ok). Should we spend that on insurance? My dad is in insurance, maybe he could help? Bad news when the truck is repaired! We just didn't sell anything. What happened with the sales department? Our total cost of goods went up too much! Are you firing people? We could do better turning off the lights. Jackson could ease the lead foot and not use so much company gas! How did we get so much bad debt?"

Whew! Finally it was over and quiet. I told them it was a good exercise, that this was the score of the game right now, that I was not firing anyone but counting on them to help me fix this. I could not have been more proud of the effort and we got the $28,000 back in three months. They knew the numbers, all of them, and that made a difference.

Benchmarking The Ideal Business

We have traveled seven *Small Business Survival 101* Principles worth which now allows us to attempt specifying the characteristics of the perfect business:

- It is something you are an expert in.
- You have no partners or investors.
- Your hardware product has 30% gross margin and requires regular service/support and supplies to make it function.
- The service/support and supply revenues are under contract.
- The product has a mundane element and is a necessity in people's lives.
- It is an outbound business and you have outside sales ability.
- You make it easy to do business and what you do makes other's lives easier. You sell easy.
- You understand accounting and get monthly financials.
- The business has a current ratio of 1.5 or higher.
- The business owner knows leadership techniques specific to small business such as treating everyone differently and "P" laws.
- Customer base is in the hundreds with 80% under contract.
- Change defense measures are deployed. Contracts short, don't own building, product line diversified, company big enough to cut back without losing it. You counterpunch.
- You made an acquisition and obtained welcome new capability, customers, cash flow.
- You hit ratio targets.

- Your overhead, including owner pay, is 100% covered by service/supply support contracts.
- Your pay is 15% of company gross profit. Owners need to be into six figures—$100,000+.

Much of the success of a business is determined by the owner's ability with numbers, his ability to process them for meaning and read the tea leaves. Your business brain can be compared to a software program because it is your operating system. Its ability to help you is only as good as the data you feed it. FEEEED it! "Being good" with figures is not an option for any business person. It is a must. By nature, as a business person, you should be used to automatically quantifying everything. Some say "I am not that good with numbers". Would you like a doctor disinterested in your blood work results and not knowing what they mean? It is just as fatal for you if you ignore your numbers.

How Big Should My Business Be?

This is a question to spend little time answering. It is good to remember that 'big' is not an accounting term. Put your time into building for stability instead of size. You know that huge companies with billions in revenue go out of business as easily as small ones. Most airlines are in this category, Lehman Bros., Enron, Hostess, Circuit City, Blockbuster, General Motors, Chrysler, and on and on. It is possible your business is better run than these. The size of the business will largely determine itself. In general, you need it big enough to throw off your desired income and to pay employees well. You want additional size to cushion against hard times if you need to cut back. If you are very small, with nowhere to cut, you may be done when hard times hit.

Over 75% of small businesses have one employee, the owner/operator. They are more rightly called self-employed or solopreneurs. Yet, this might be a professional athlete with a 15 million a year salary or an independent welder making $70,000. That is about the range, the high and the low, for a one man band. Do you see size of a company having any bearing in this example? You could dial up or down any combination of size and pay.

I will give you my experience. At our peak we needed numerous technicians because copiers broke frequently. I had 45 employees including an office in another city and two copy shops.

Advancements began to make copiers more reliable needing less service. Simultaneously, laser printers became as fast as copiers and took "clicks" from copiers. Change! Change! Change! The good news was copiers required less parts and labor so as revenue and headcount dropped, the expense dropped with it, leaving the company with familiar gross profit—the important number. We also learned to work on laser printers. My pay was in six figures.

Years went by and the copier market matured and did not grow. It became less profitable and I reduced expenses, renegotiated loans and leases, and sought lower prices to compensate. I compensated by making an acquisition to replace lost revenue. My pay stayed the same. After the GR swept through, I had a smaller company but pay stayed close to the same which surprised even me. So size is less a factor because it is more about running efficiently. The SBA defines a small business as under 6 million in revenue if a retail or service business or under $500,000 if agricultural. Only 4% of businesses have 10+ employees according to Forbes magazine.

Here is a thought on our times. The country has very high unemployment around 8% meaning 21,000,000 are jobless. There are 28,000,000 small businesses so if each hired one person this would wipe out unemployment. But 'full' employment is considered 3% unemployment so if only half of small businesses could hire a new worker the economy would suddenly buzz. That is the power of the small business sector but the fact it cannot do this speaks to its weak state.

Of our 28 million establishments that are called small businesses (many quite loosely) only 6 million have paid employees according to both the U.S. Census and the Kauffman foundation. In my opinion those are the ones to be called businesses. The others may be no more the equivalent of an online manicure service or somebody owning and operating a pay phone but they still go into the stats as a small business.

Your Pay

A business owner can make a six figure income from a million dollar business if built in a methodically profitable way from the beginning. Typical owner salary is 10-12% of annual revenues. The IRS says the average pay for the average 'S' corporation with 1.5 million in revenue is 100,000. Sub chapter S corporations are generally more profitable than sole proprietorships.

The cautionary tale for a growing businesses is that it takes more of you. Only you can determine what is enough but business success at the expense of family, friends, health or faith is not real success. If you work, then go home and then back to work you have a problem. If you have the uncommon problem of a business getting big make sure it is on your terms and those close to you. To do that successfully delegate and hire right. This is the long term strategy to work yourself out of a job which, in turn, lets you retire.

It is important to put your pay into the budget as a regular line item no matter what. I repeat. No matter what. Owners sometimes have the mentality of 'taking a check' when the money seems to be there. That is not the way to do it. Success in business is about discipline as much as anything. You discipline yourself to pay things like the rent, utilities and payroll taxes on time and regularly which is exactly why they get paid. It is just a groove in your financial hard drive and you need to treat your pay the same.

You have a lot to deal with and your own pay should not be one of those things but rather something that helps you deal with the other things. There are plenty of books about 'as a man thinketh so he is' and 'we are what we think we are' and all that. There is a lot of truth to them so think you are supposed to get a regular paycheck and you will. Sure, there can be a few times you wait a bit on it but that should be it. Your pay is part of the overhead and needs to be listed near the top.

Congratulations! You can remove your oxygen mask. You have done so well with the numbers that you made it to Chapter 8, the last one.

Moe's summation: "Everyone knows we can't work a calculator but we excel at important things. Nobody matches us for loyalty, undivided attention, listening, unconditional caring, dedication, responsiveness and alertness. These traits build great businesses too. But I am glad my owner has my number."

8 Have An Exit Plan

This is not a chapter on IRAs or 401Ks. It is on your mental state. At some point into your, ahem, later years as a business owner, into your late forties or fifties, some things occur to you 1) You do not have the passion and drive you used to 2) You want a way to exit or modify that leaves you with something and 3) you want space to do something else. You are well aware of the twenty and thirty year olds coming that possess the energy ethic you had plus they understand the bits, bytes and blinking lights of current technology.

How do you compete? You don't is that answer. You hire it. This is not an easy transition and may not even be possible given the difficulty of this time but if you want to power down you will certainly have to counter this with people who can power up. Have the foresight to plan for this in some way so you may be able to reap a decent harvest. The middle ages of a business and its owner are dangerous. Very dangerous.

Passion and drive always kept things percolating but what if they just aren't there like they used to be for whatever reason? Certain jobs call out for certain retirement ages. If a pilot, it is mandatory at 65. If an NFL running back it may be 35. A business owner would not be living as intensely as an NFL running back but more so than an airline pilot so your play out is in between those two ages. The regular play in business ownership involves a lot of creativity, coping with difficulty, problems solving, personnel management, cash flow management and all the rest. None of these have cut and dry solutions and call for the owner's maximum nuclear power output to resolve. That process burns a lot more uranium than say an algebra teacher who deals with a known, unchanging fixed universe. It all depends on what you have to give to it to be at maximum effectiveness. If there is no plan or adjustment for your life's state, you slowly ruin the business, driving down its value and your own well-being. You know the joke: How do you end up with a small fortune in small business? Start with a large one! You don't want that to be you.

I hate to say this but this is my weakest chapter and the last one. And for good reason, because, as I have shouted, "You can't give what you don't have!" I do not have the comprehensive knowledge of this step that I do the others. But I am, in fact, in it, so that should help. I don't even like being in it to be honest. I am 62 and tired of doing the same thing for 35 years. Should this section then be better entitled Epilogue or Epitaph instead of Chapter 8? Oh no, having to decide between such terms (short for terminal?) like these. I have to realize I am nearing the opposite end of the rainbow. Is there a pot of gold or just a pot of old? Help! We are certainly a long way from Kansas and days of starting a business.

I am thankful I still have an income from my business but it has declined some as I have backed off. I find my most significant thought, other than survival, is finding something more meaningful to do. I am still looking. A friend directed me to a national guidance group called "Halftime" whose motto is "Moving from success to significance." This states my dilemma well and shows I am not alone. So boo hoo for me. I have to deal with this stage just like any other stage of ownership along the way. So deal! In his mega-selling book *The Seven Habits of Highly Effective People* Stephen Covey speaks of beginning something with the end in mind and that is good advice for a long term owner.

Most small businesses are lifestyle business that form uniquely around owners' habits, hours, hobbies and preferences. Regardless of how the business is doing owners still get a lot of enjoyment living as they have styled it and only as a business owner can. As you work out of the business, work hard to keep these important things in your life because they have been your life.

"It becomes about profit and profit not profit and loss."

Touchdown! What, AARP sends you membership cards at 50?! Oh no, is it over? Well, some of it might be but comes a time when the business needs to serve you instead of the other way around— where you are mostly doing things you like and leaving the rest for other pay grades. Where it is about profit and profit instead of profit and loss. I love my company, my 15 employees, and the relationships it gives me. I no longer like hearing about disgruntled customers, a lost sale, why a customer cancelled, how we lost money this month, how we need to hire a better employee, somebody not paying, and on and on. Which makes me a bad leader, really. Then again, it's understandable, because ownership is a more demanding lifestyle than non-ownership.

I love how Stephen McDonnell, president of an 80 employee company, puts this. He says he tries not to go into the office much anymore, maybe twice a week, and work from home. "I think you can observe what's happening so much easier from the outside than when you are inside it. Your whole outlook changes. You actually become a therapist to your organization. When you are inside it you are the patient." Brilliantly put. I still want to be in the owner's box but move up from the playing field, helping determine strategy, profitability, and work with a few close people who get me and get things done. That is my plan. Which means someone else has to become part of my plan to do what I won't, errrr, don't.

I passed opportunities to sell years ago because the buyer required I lay off seven people to do it. Not me. I made the decision to ride as far as it will take me and my faithful. If it were to tank then I shall tank with them. If I am worth a darn then I should be able to strategize wisely enough to keep on. Which I have, so far, even in this recession. I still have my income and a decent life of which I am boss, just how I like it. Yet, I still have work to do to figure out the next ten years. I have maybe 25 and do not want to spend more than I have to worrying about selling things. Somewhere things will go on without me—some are now—yet still getting my subsistence. And it is six figures so I have to be about it. As Cindy says: "Show me the money!" That is what this eighth principle is about, discerning your retirement money. You didn't come this far to have nothing so let's look at exit strategies.

Selling vs. Keeping

It is likely that as you do less, or want to, company value goes down with this motivational change. Your enterprise got where it did, conquered all, because you were steering. If there is no one to replace you as helmsman, and the business continues to slowly decline dropping value, then selling is always a consideration. This in itself takes planning and at least six months to a year to do right. I will get to the business valuation but the net proceeds from a sale will be the equivalent of four to five years of salary/benefits. That is just how it works out.

For the sale option to work this amount needs to carry you, and it might, since you reduced household overhead down by now, right? More likely, this stash, along with supplemental income, gets it done. Social Security may help with the supplemental income. I get full payment, about $2700, at 66, as it stands, no matter how much I make. You can begin drawing at 62, maybe a maximum of $1500, but even that is reduced and can be entirely eliminated if you are still earning a certain amount of other income.

To sell a business you need very accurate financial statements and tax returns. To me, only the last year matters but prior years give the trends. The highest price comes from someone in your industry folding in your business under his roof. This cuts total overhead of the two combined companies and makes them more profitable than standing separately.

The purchase price is based upon re-casted cash flow-what the free cash flow is after the two are combined and after removing all your pay and benefits as well as all debt service. The buyer will try to decrease this amount saying he has to charge something for the use of his building, staff and assets and he has a point. He will use 'net present value' accounting to decrease the value of the business each year by 5-10% to account for depreciation of the assets he bought. You counter saying they were not being fully utilized and you bringing in your company fixes that and therefore nothing should be deducted. Good luck to both!

Negotiations work best if the owner does not conduct them. Let your accountant or attorney hold the initial talks and you come in later. This will get you a higher price and save sanity during the process which preserves brain neurons which, in turn, preserves purchase proceeds. Most companies sell for 3 to 5 times the agreed upon annual re-casted free cash flow. Real estate and inventory is always separate. You will have to pay debt off from the proceeds. You keep your current assets and current liabilities as of the closing date. There should be more gain there since current assets are usually higher than current liabilities providing you collect the AR and can sell the inventory.

It should work out that you pay the low long term capital gains tax on the proceeds which is 15%. You may choose to carry a note, maybe 30%, which delays paying taxes on this amount and earns income by charging interest. Most sales are not all cash anyway, and banks only loan 2.5 times positive cash flow, so plan on financing some of the purchase. Normally, the seller stays at least six months, or longer, to help the transition, and is paid for, but that is entirely negotiable. It goes without saying that your business needs to be able to carry on without you and the new owner has the expertise to take over.

Keeping It

Keeping the business is the most profitable route if you can back away and retain your salary. If you can keep it up for four or five years you will have earned about the same as from a sale. Now sell it! Maybe not.

Hopefully you have enough younger trained hands that can carry on and keep mailing you a check. Or, you have a selected heir who slowly buys you over some period. It is important to have something else to do if you do get out. I am slowly backing out as I can but find I get bored easier than I used to. I think I am *backing away* from the business demands, which I am fine with, but still looking for more things to *go forward to* which I do not have in place. Writing is filling some of that and my woodworking hobby. I still enjoy my contact with my company so I guess it is a pretty good plan. But, I think I have found I do not like having to have a plan for this!

I think you have to plan five years out from your D-Day. You should start an exit plan when you find yourself, well, exiting. By this I mean find yourself cutting out earlier, having less contact with your peeps and customers, become bored with the business, and just making do. You have not innovated much, displayed at trade shows, hired new blood, taken on new products or territory, quit educating yourself, and the like. You have, in effect, begun retiring. At least from your current business. This may not be occurring during the traditional retirement zone and could come before that. This frame is going to cost you a lot of money so the sooner you recognize it, and change something, the better.

T.E.N.E.s

At a business consulting school this syndrome was discussed. The speaker said entrepreneurs can lose passion for running a business because they much more enjoy launching one as well as mulling new ideas in one. The presenter said entrepreneurs start a business, and sustain one too, by regular TENEs which stood for Temporary Entrepreneurial Neuron Explosions. These are entrepreneur's equivalents of the Big Bang Theory that began the universe only they begin new ventures. TENEs drive people to call themselves 'serial entrepreneurs' who need, too frequently, another juicing.

The term concerns me. If you are leaving one failed business for another then you are not a serial entrepreneur but trying to become a real one for the first time. If you had businesses, sustained them, and sold for a profit then claim the title. But once these TENEs, whether big or very small cease, it is like Superman being hit by kryptonite because drive, energy and passion are sapped. This produces an unwelcome fork in the road and you know Yogi's Fork Rule: "When you come to a fork in the road you should take it." Just about that clear for sure.

Some at this juncture start another business, possibly a good idea. I have done it and it got me out of a rut at 50 when I started Kawasaki of Memphis and sold eight years later. I remember discussing this move with my CPA who specializes in small businesses and been my CPA from the beginning. I told him I thought I may be 'burnt out' because I just did not enjoy it like I used to. He asked me an important question: "Do you still want to work?" "Absolutely," I responded. "I would love to have something to dig into whereas now I just preside." Then the wise Ed said "you are not burnt out then." And I wasn't. It is a certainty that this fork calls for new rocket fuel from somewhere. The best places are your interests and hobbies, anything that holds your attention today. You do best what you *like* to do. New directions hinge on finances, too, which vary all over the place. You have to approach a new venture with all you learned from your career, plus the eight principles in *Small Business Survival 101*. I think the wise man puts more and more time in areas of satisfaction and tries to slowly remove those that are noise. Slowly remove overhead while you are at it. Then you may well be rid of profit and loss and move to profit and profit, the final success.

Time is of some essence. Remember that 20% of customer base in play each year. That means customers are moving out, downsizing, closing up, switching to another vendor or selling their business. Just the usual turnover. You have to fight to keep that number in single digits while adding new customers. This takes nuclear effort in a down economy. My point is that if you want to 'rest' on your customer base, hoping it will hold you, it will only do so for a while and not a long while. If you did not add one new customer in these five years then turnover statistics say you would have lost all your customers. Thus, if energy for developing new business has waned you will not keep your customer base and deterioration accelerates further threatening retirement. Losing even 20% of your base could be enough to end the business.

Short Term Exit

There are circumstances where a short term exit plan may be appropriate. If you are in a volatile business, say retail, restaurant or high tech, you likely will not be in that to retirement. That is what the statistics say. Just rapidly changing tech or a new competitor moving into the marketplace, or your zip code going into decline, can be enough to take down these type businesses. It doesn't mean it will be yours, of course. It may be that your business has reached its peak, will never be worth more, and you want to cash in while you can. Recognizing you are in the vulnerable zone keep an exit plan developed at all times. Maybe it is someone bigger who could buy you out if trouble strikes. It may be a plan to slowly close down. Advance planning could go a long way to keeping you from losing it all.

Partial Exit

If you have a business of say at least 15 employees you may be able to work a partial exit by keeping just a piece of the business you could work that throws off meaningful recurring income. Maybe you keep a few techs and proportionate service revenue and do some selling yourself. This arrangement should provide time to enjoy or pursue other interests like a hobby or business. Doing this would decrease your purchase price but the return is that the piece you keep will likely stay going past a five year payout for all your business and thus make you the most money long term.

As you work your exit try to get the purchaser to agree to small things that could be big to you or at least things you would have to pay for in the future. You get to use his warehouse, borrow the lift gate truck when you need it, forward your calls to his switchboard when you vacation. Maybe there is agreement to micro borrow collection people or accounting people to file things for you for an appropriate payment saving you from hiring someone. You could still be listed as an employee to stay on group insurance.

I'm Exiting

It ends here. I mean this book. That leaves this chapter unfinished which is right where I am too. I am not qualified to write any further or I would be trying to give you something I do not have.

Moe's summation: "I don't know where my boss is trying to go here but wherever it is I am going with him. That said I don't ever think about exits and such but instead enjoy living in the moment."

Afterword

Thanks for reading! I hope the *Small Business Survival 101* lessons, sayings and declarations ring in your head for months to come to your great benefit.

For two years I was a weekly columnist for *The Memphis Daily News,* a daily business paper in Memphis. I went under the title "The Small Business Adviser" and published over 100 columns on the life of a small business owner as well as putting forth some advice. What follows are reprints of a few of my favorite Small Business Adviser columns.

In addition I have put forth a list of what I consider the top reasons for business failures.

Men Untied Over Ties

By Tom Pease

Seems some businessmen are abandoning ties. I think it is a mistake. The look of no tie and open collar looks unprofessional and reduces confidence. It looks like something is missing which may be your image. What is the message? "My ease is more important than respect for you?" Or, "I realize I am too powerful looking in my suit and tie so I am toning myself down?"

Clothes Make the Man is a mantra of many men. Esquire and GQ magazines still love suits and ties. Dress for Success is still taught. Women have never given up looking their best. What's the deal?

We expect professionals to look the part, at least during business hours. This provides the public reassurance. We still want the judge in robes, lawyers in ties, police in blue, clergy with a collar, military with fatigues, and pilots with shoulder strips and caps . We would be dismayed if the judge showed in a bathrobe, police in tank tops, a soldier in a jogging suit, pilots in sweatshirts and clergy in pajamas, although these things may be near.

Most "authorities" wear ties. Must be reasons such as looking the part, looking confident. News bulletin: customers do not want you to look like them. They want you to represent a higher authority, knowledge or stature, and dress should communicate that. Why diminish it? Those dressing too casual for business may be spending more time with themselves and their ideas than with customers.

There is thought that says look like your customer, don't be too stiff. OK. Don't look like a "suit" I guess. If so, shouldn't you ditch the suit instead of the tie? And some do. The tie is aptly named in that it ties together the rest of the triad of shirt and coat. Eliminate the tie and things just don't tie together. If you insist on going tieless consider going without the coat. Wear French cuffs to show some class. Shoes shined. Wear a suit coat with the straight collar and no button down collar. A pocket square helps. If you cannot project confidence customers perceive you don't have any. Yes, Steve Jobs wore jeans, and Zuckerberg a hoody, but you are not them. Wearing a button down collar (undershirt showing ?!) blazer and contrasting pants has the look of an eighth grade geometry teacher. Perhaps that is the goal-to look academic- but it makes one look somewhat tired in my opinion. Part of the casualness may be we are overweight and lack confidence in our clothes. A tailor helps.

The best dress shows the most respect for customers, that is number one. One thought I have on the statement, or lack of one, the tie-less are sending is that they do not feel they carry the image for their company anymore because their knock out website, blog, You Tube and the like do that. I met with someone trying to sell me something who was well dressed. I wore shirt but no tie or coat on a day off. When I arrived, I was miffed that he immediately took off his tie! Why? Weird. He had a gold watch too, and I did not, but he didn't remove that. Rule: in front of customers wear your best stuff. If chumming with peers or after hours, then whatever.

How many are for cravats and how many against? It may come down to a tie.

What Small Business Needs Now
By TOM PEASE
Special to The Daily News

My banker called and wanted my annual financial statement. I asked if he still had last year's, and he did, so I told him take 25% off everything on that. This reflects the drop in my business as well as real estate . I feel this is representative of others like me or close.

There is nothing bringing back that 25% anytime soon. We can meet about it, talk about it, form committees, network groups , ask the government for a handout, cheer lead it, but these do not address the problem. The real problem is sizable demand and customer traffic have vaporized in the wake of consumers' drop in net worth . Gone. Evaporated. The consumer has no meaningful discretionary money and that grows the economy. Plan accordingly.

So the pie is smaller which means everyone gets a smaller piece. For there to be growth the pie has to come out of the oven bigger. Not only that, but people demand ice cream with it. There have been no U.S. chefs that know how to bake it. In some cases, pies have become cupcakes. In other cases, the oven has been shut down.

The sad truth of this economy may be that it is the new normal and we have recovered all we are going to. I hope not but it is easy to make this case. Unemployment won't move from 9%. Home values are at their lowest. There is no money to earn in a savings account. Jobs moved overseas. The government has a negative net worth. Empty commercial buildings abound. In 2008 *Inc.* magazine said 595,600 businesses closed . Wow. That is 11,900 per state. Raises are scarce and credit card limits reduced. Where is the lost 25% going to come? How do you put dust back in the ground?

If all factors normalized tomorrow it would still take years to replenish the 25%.

A recession benefit has been low prices. You hear this is cheap and that is cheap. Not really. It is just what it is worth now. Maybe lower prices will help even out lower spending power.

The reason the economy deflated badly is because it never was as robust as it appeared. In hindsight we see that is because crucial segments of it, such as housing, banking, and the federal government itself, were Ponzi operations. They used pseudo profits to make more pseudo profits. Bernie Madoff stuff. We know what happens on that day of reckoning: nothing. The money is gone. That is where we are. How to recover nobody really knows.

The country has been "rightsized." It had tremendous waste and pointless consumption that did nothing to build our foundations to be more efficient, like other countries, so we are paying the price of work going to China etc.

If a small businessman owned the government I know he'd cut 10% now from everyone getting a government check. Everyone. He would require those receiving unemployment to earn it by working free for a small business some and contribute to the economy. Send all military sitting around on bases in other countries to Afghanistan to end that thing. And importantly, make a Cabinet position for Small Business.

Tom Pease is owner of e/Doc Systems and author of "Going Out of Business By Design: Why 70% of Small Businesses Fail."

7/7/10

Your New Vocabulary

By Tom Pease

Small business owners have their own unique world of pain and problems. You may not have known it, but new terms have come to describe them. If you have had a hard time finding the right words, check this list.

Winning Ugly. What you are doing now. Visiting uncomfortable areas you never have to make profit such as rent concession , paying sales tax with credit card, reducing pay and hours, demanding vendors lower prices, refinancing loans or leases, taking a penalty to help cash, dialing for dollars, being a cheapskate. Whacking. Cutting. Buying groceries at Aldi.

Screen Vision. Addictive and incurable condition. When you realize you spend more time in front of screens than customers.

TENE. Temporary Entrepreneurial Neuron Explosion. Plagues entrepreneurs when they begin living off next big idea instead of making present one work. Just the thing though for bored owners.

It's a Mona Lisa. When it looks good only on paper or in the eye of the beholder.

Time Vampires. Tasks that owners get tied up in that should be delegated.

Job. Leading US export. Something where the U.S. leads China.

Mind Ninja. When you are being mentally overwhelmed or overwhelming someone else.

Cash No. Because you don't have any. It goes out as fast as it comes in. Term replaces Cash Flow. You remember—when revenue grew a bit, customers paid on time, you did too, and banks loaned some.

Psychic Income. Term used by the President of Coca-Cola to describe the enjoyment in non-cash rewards of a job.

Bipolar Disorder. Closely describes the up then down mental state experienced by owners. Also descriptive of the suddenness of the mood swings.

Deciding While Intoxicated. This is business DWI and occurs when there is too much ego involved in decision making. Most prevalent in men. Customers get it too. These decisions come undone.

Sales Menopause. When our business warrior gets into the forties passion and initiative to go out and get new business wane. Best to plan for this and move to a management position where wisdom and instinct are needed most.

Walking Between Raindrops. Braving through the week trying to avoid getting hit by bad news.

Eating and Drinking. Hopefully what your products do. No, this has nothing to do with a restaurant. It means when you sell your products they produce a residual revenue stream such as service, support or supplies, that gets you through.

Pinballing. Staying in play, bouncing off one prospect after another as long as possible, until you light up for a score. Means one thing leads to another. Keep moving!

Change Monster. A force that devours businesses. Picture a Tyrannosaurus Rex with huge jaws hovered over your business wanting to destroy it. May be out there right now. Change is a certainty in business. It is coming. Change, or the monster eats.

Sales Prevention Unit. Admins that gets carried away with command and control. Yes, sales people are unwieldy but they think you are too. Work together or lose business.

Treating Everyone Differently. Best management method for a small business.

Going Out of Business By Design. Setting in motion a business built on poor strategy destined to fail.

Entrepreneurship By Santa Claus. Wantapreneurs or entrepreneurs who expect to be handed business or capital for reasons other than earning it.

Summary of Top Reasons Businesses Fail

Owner Ignorance. Owner not prepared. Lack of necessary background. Does not get regular vital information and adjust quickly. Poor controls.

Selling Wrong Product. Does not eat and drink. Cannot be put under contract. Easily made obsolete.

Pricing Inadequate. Too low. Never raised. Too variable.

Passion Lost. Drive and passion played out. Creative element missing. Available horsepower not enough.

Bad Leadership. Boss cannot get the most from employees. Does not treat everyone differently. Reclusive. Doesn't know employees. Does not ensure morale.

DWI. Deciding while intoxicated on ego. These decisions come undone. Are poorly thought out.

Focus On Revenue and Not GP. Tracking gross profit is the tell tale figure, not revenue.

Poor Use of Owner's Time. Not enough time on "A" tasks.

Law Of Negativity. Owner's energy and employee morale sapped by terminal negativity.

Partners. Partnerships are based on need more than want. Eventually a problem. Can blow up the business.

Change Monster. You have been visited by Businessaurus Rex and he is munching on your business. No change … no change.

Business Mismatched To Personality. The demands are a mismatch to the way you like to work and like to work on.

No Stress Management. Addicted to the business and can't get away from it. It runs you instead of you running it. No physical work outs. You and family burn down.

Not Keeping Up With Tech. You lost opportunities for you business to run better. Also causes you to lag behind understanding how your customers work.

The Great Recession. Enough said! A lot of company.

About The Author

Tom Pease is semi-retired as the 33 year owner of e/Doc Systems Inc. a Memphis office equipment dealership. During this time his companies produced 110 million dollars in revenue. He has published over 100 columns as the Small Business Advisor for the Memphis Daily News. He is author of Going Out of Business By Design—Why 70% of Small Businesses Fail. He was the recipient of the Memphis Small Business Executive Of The Year in 1994.

Tom also started Kawasaki of Memphis in 1999, a full line power sports dealership that rose to the top 15% in the country and sold it eight years later.

Tom has a degree in Communications from the University of Tennessee and enjoys any kind of vehicle and working on his farm with his donkey Dusty and dogs Moe (co-author), Atticus and Scout. He is married to Cindy Speros Pease and has two children, Parker and Lacey and Decs, his grandchild.

He is a member of St. Ann Catholic Church in Bartlett, TN and lives in Gallaway, TN.

Contact him at tcivlj@aol.com or 901-367-9500.

14 487906